Cambridge Elements

Elements in Theatre, Performance and the Political
edited by
Trish Reid
University of Reading
Liz Tomlin
University of Glasgow

EMPIRE, EXTRACTION AND POWER IN THE FESTIVALS OF BRITAIN OF 1951 AND 2022

Caoimhe Mader McGuinness
Kingston University London

Shaftesbury Road, Cambridge CB2 8EA, United Kingdom

One Liberty Plaza, 20th Floor, New York, NY 10006, USA

477 Williamstown Road, Port Melbourne, VIC 3207, Australia

314–321, 3rd Floor, Plot 3, Splendor Forum, Jasola District Centre, New Delhi – 110025, India

103 Penang Road, #05–06/07, Visioncrest Commercial, Singapore 238467

Cambridge University Press is part of Cambridge University Press & Assessment, a department of the University of Cambridge.

We share the University's mission to contribute to society through the pursuit of education, learning and research at the highest international levels of excellence.

www.cambridge.org
Information on this title: www.cambridge.org/9781009461252

DOI: 10.1017/9781009461269

© Caoimhe Mader McGuinness 2025

This publication is in copyright. Subject to statutory exception and to the provisions of relevant collective licensing agreements, no reproduction of any part may take place without the written permission of Cambridge University Press & Assessment.

When citing this work, please include a reference to the DOI 10.1017/9781009461269

First published 2025

A catalogue record for this publication is available from the British Library

ISBN 978-1-009-46125-2 Hardback
ISBN 978-1-009-46128-3 Paperback
ISSN 2753-1244 (online)
ISSN 2753-1236 (print)

Cambridge University Press & Assessment has no responsibility for the persistence or accuracy of URLs for external or third-party internet websites referred to in this publication and does not guarantee that any content on such websites is, or will remain, accurate or appropriate.

For EU product safety concerns, contact us at Calle de José Abascal, 56, 1°, 28003 Madrid, Spain, or email eugpsr@cambridge.org

Empire, Extraction and Power in the Festivals of Britain of 1951 and 2022

Elements in Theatre, Performance and the Political

DOI: 10.1017/9781009461269
First published online: November 2025

Caoimhe Mader McGuinness
Kingston University London
Author for correspondence: Caoimhe Mader McGuinness,
c.madermcguinness@kingston.ac.uk

Abstract: This Element compares the 1951 Festival of Britain with the 2022 Unboxed Festival to explore both continuities and shifts in the British state's relationship to empire, power and extraction as expressed in celebrations of national culture. The ideological projects underpinning these governments, distanced by more than seventy years, might be seen as fundamentally opposed. Yet approaching this comparative study through a conjunctural analysis focusing on the narrations of British identity and both events' wilful intertwining of technology and art reveals the continuities between both periods, especially as they pertain to historical practices of the imperial state and its far-reaching consequences.

Keywords: festivals, performance, extraction, empire, power

© Caoimhe Mader McGuinness 2025

ISBNs: 9781009461252 (HB), 9781009461283 (PB), 9781009461269 (OC)
ISSNs: 2753-1244 (online), 2753-1236 (print)

Contents

1 Introduction   1

2 Bordered Identities   18

3 Extractive Labours   35

4 Improvement: Land to Outer Space   52

5 Conclusion   69

   References   72

1 Introduction

In unearthing testimonies about the 1951 Festival of Britain (FOB), a recurring motif is the awe felt at arriving at the fully revamped Southbank across the still bombed out landscapes of early 1950s London. Chief among the marvels encountered, the Skylon reigns supreme. One of the most iconic structures of the event, the Skylon was designed by young architects Hidalgo Moya and Philip Powell, a seemingly gravity-defying contraption shooting up into the London sky well above the other temporary structures of the festival. A metal oblong space age cigar-shaped structure fixed upon four spider-like legs, it appeared to float upwards to demonstrate – according to Richard Hornsey – 'the romantic potentialities of twentieth century building science' (2010: 6). Nothing remains of this impressive structure, only referenced now in the name of a restaurant atop the Royal Festival Hall, itself the only structure which has in fact endured since 1951. Various rumours circulated regarding what had become of it, most prominently that it had been thrown into the river Thames by the subsequent hostile Conservative government led by Winston Churchill which had continually raised questions about the festival's costs. It was in fact simply sent to the scrap heap. Yet the Skylon is central to popular memories of the festival, including a commemorative documentary aired on the BBC in 2011 in which one of its visitors recalls a recurring joke from the period: 'Like the British economy, it had no visible means of support' (Hendy, 2011).

The 1951 festival of Britain emerged as the brainchild of Herbert Morrison around 1947, then Labour MP for Lewisham East and Leader of the House of Commons. Originally conceived as a commemoration of the 1851 Great Exhibition, the festival quickly began to emerge as something rather quite different in scale and focus, not least due to Britain's much trickier historical position regarding straightforward celebrations of empire which the 1851 display had more squarely been. However, what it may not have been in a position to replicate in terms of geopolitical centrality, it made up for in scale, benefitting from a budget of £12 million (equivalent to approximately £322 million today). Indeed, while the 1951 festival is often memorialised as having occurred primarily on the South Bank of London did in fact extend across many territories, from larger scale projects such as the Ulster Farm and Factories Exhibition held in the North of Ireland to the Industrial Power Exhibition held in Glasgow. The festival also included two travelling exhibitions, one by boat on the HMS *Campania*, the other by land as well as locally organised celebrations and pageants held in cities and towns across the country.

One key feature underpinning the festival was to showcase a harmonious collaboration between art and science, in parts driven, according to Becky Conekin by an anxiety around the excesses of science seen in the Second World War and how these may be tempered by collaborations with the arts and humanities. Conversely, she also notes that 'while the South Bank structures aestheticized the scientific future, the festival also sought to enlist science as the foundation of a new modernist aesthetic' (2003: 57). Yet insofar as a larger amount of literature has focused on how the festival represented British identity, it appears that throughout the main exhibits, art mostly played a supporting role in rendering narrations of national progress innovatively accessible. Most prominently, this supporting role was evident in the modernist design of the South Bank's pavilions and their displays, which alongside the Exhibition of Science in Kensington narrated versions of Britain's past, present and possible futures. These separate exhibits focused on a range of topics such as Health, Homes and Gardens, or Sea and Ships, organised upstream and downstream around the centrepiece Dome of Discovery. This large circular structure which served as a visual inspiration for the Blair-era Millennium Dome contained the largest display on the South Bank, taking visitors on an exploration of Britain's natural and geological history all the way to outer space. The numerous other pavilions' styles were mostly airy and open, inspired by Scandinavian mid-century architecture, with facades of glass inviting visitors into their respective topical and often interactive displays. Further West visitors could enjoy the Battersea Pleasure Gardens, the only official festival event dedicated wholly to leisure and the only festival event squarely grounded in resolutely nostalgic understandings of Britain, borrowing from eighteenth-century landscaping and Victorian popular entertainment aesthetics. Meanwhile to the East in Poplar stood 'a live exhibition' which showcased the newly built Lansbury estate including one show flat as part of a wider appraisal of post-war Town Planning and Building Research. The Land Travelling Exhibition, housed in an enormous mobile metal structure travelled to the manufacturing cities of Manchester, Leeds, Birmingham and Nottingham. Describing the exhibit as nearly too modern and cosmopolitan, a 1951 *Guardian* review notes its tailored focus on the 'British people and the things they make' (Shrapnel, 1951). This concern for showcasing production also translated into the actual display of workers across the sites of the Ulster, South Bank and Glasgow exhibitions. I will discuss the latter as one of my three case studies from the festival, with further sections focusing on the Sea Travelling Exhibition and the South Bank's Lion and Unicorn Pavilion. However, I hope this attempt to give some indication of the diverse but interconnected strands at the heart of the FOB's displays give a certain sense of its thematic and aesthetic concerns. Underpinned by a modernist futurism tethered to persistent references to the past, the festival presented a sense of national pride in Britain's historical and contemporary role in developing new technologies, expressed both at the grander scale of scientific progress in gestures towards outer space, atomic energy and ships as well through a more quotidian focus on modern architecture and design, technology and commodity production.

Unboxed 2022 was announced by then prime minister Theresa May in September 2018. Originally planned for 2021, seventy years after the FOB, she announced a 'nationwide festival in celebration of the creativity and innovation of the United Kingdom' (Buchan, 2018). Explicitly comparing the proposed project to the 1951 festival as well as the Great Exhibition, she declared that 'Almost 70 years ago the Festival of Britain stood as a symbol of change. Britain once again stands on the cusp of a new future as an outward facing global trading nation. Just as millions of Britons celebrated their nation's great achievements in 1951, we want to showcase what makes our country great today' (Buchan, 2018). What was to become Unboxed 2022: Creativity in the UK was beleaguered by questions about its purpose, becoming colloquially known as the Festival of Brexit after a quip by former far-right Conservative MP Jacob Rees-Mogg. Throughout its inception it was challenged from the left by the group Migrants in Culture noting its xenophobic links to Brexit and from the right for its £120 million cost and the perceived unseriousness of some of its projects. As Unboxed developed, however, it became clear that it would be far from any explicit celebration of Brexit. Led by Martin Green, who also oversaw the 2012 Olympics ceremonies, its website describes the festival as presenting '10 awe-inspiring new ideas, shaped across science, technology, engineering, the arts and mathematics by brilliant minds working in unexpected collaborations' (*Our Place in Space*). Grouped under the new acronym STEAM, reminiscent of the joining of arts and science championed by the FOB, it consisted of ten separate events dotted across Britain and the North of Ireland. According to a disparaging review by Stuart McGurk in the House magazine, at least one of the projects teams demanded the word Brexit be explicitly not be mentioned in their work (2022). Alongside questions about cost and attendance numbers, many conservative MPs expressed dissatisfaction with the project on ideological grounds, seeing a missed opportunity to not actually make the festival an opportunity to celebrate Britain's eventual exit from the EU. Yet it was also still being defended in September 2022 by the then arts secretary Stephen Parkinson as a means to bring people together: 'Whether that's post-Brexit, thinking about what unites us, or post-pandemic, getting people back out of their houses, or indeed cost-of-living, where it's giving people something joyful and inspiring ... ' (McGurk, 2022). Nevertheless, an investigation into cost and attendance was launched, revealing it had grossed £175.5 million in monetisable benefits and that a live and digital audiences of twenty million did in fact engage with the festival, a moderate success despite the criticism received and unshakeable Festival of Brexit misnomer.

Despite the direct link made by Theresa May between both festivals, the purpose of Unboxed 2022 was less grounded in representing the nation to itself but rather to showcase Britain's creativity to itself. This took the shape of ten discrete projects, all grounded in specific collaborations between science and/or technology and the arts and none of these took the shape of a conventional exhibition such as those presented at the FOB. Only two of the projects took a time-based form and most work often, if not always, was presented across a range of media such as phone apps, websites, Virtual Reality (VR) headsets and television. Given the prevalence of the climate crisis in public discourse, alongside the very recent experience of lockdowns across the island, sustainability, the natural world and ecology became recurring sources of inspiration across many projects, although these took many different shapes. *Dandelion*, a collaboration between multi-disciplinary arts collective Approxima, the James Hutton Institute alongside Celtic Music organisations, was predicated on community sowing and growing of plants across Scotland, alongside the creation of LED lit 'garden cubes' and two free music festivals. Meanwhile, *Green Space Dark Skies*, a collaboration between outdoor arts production company Walk the Plank and community arts organisation Activate, sought to celebrate 'our right to roam', enrolling people local to twelve national parks across the country to create 'extraordinary outdoor artworks with their lights – captured on camera in a series of beautiful and powerful short films' (Unboxed). *Pollinations* created an urban garden in Birmingham and developed a phone application using augmented reality (AR) to enable users to plant a flower anywhere and watch it grow in real time. The climate crisis was also a focus of *Seemonster* and to a lesser degree *About Us*, two projects I will discuss in further sections, which took extractive infrastructure and the interconnection between humans and the cosmos as their respective starting points.

The other recurring thematic was a sense of futurism sometimes intertwined with outer space. *Dreamachine*, saw the artist collective Assemble team up with neuroscientists to build a sensory immersive experience conjuring personal a luminous and technicolour internal kaleidoscopic world enabled by lying with one's eyes closed, surrounded by flickering light and sound (Dreamachine). *Our Place in Space* saw visual artist and illustrator Oliver Jeffers work with astrophysicist Stephen Smartt and creative media arts organisation Nerve Centre to create a sculpture trail supported by an augmented reality phone application which took visitors for an educational walk through the solar system. *GALWAD*, a collaboration including but not limited to National Theatre Wales, Disability Arts Cymru and Ffilm Cymru, developed a series of live streamed performances broadcast over a week online alongside a companion piece on Sky Arts which imagined a speculative scenario in which an electrical storm enables contact between individuals from 2022 and 2052. Finally, *Tour de Moon* offered an extensive range of events created by a similarly extensive range of collaborators which included Magid Magid, former Mayor of Sheffield, designer Nelly Ben Hayoun-Stépanian and president of WeTransfer Damian Bradfield. This project travelled through English cities and organised three-day festivals celebrating nightlife and counterculture as a means to imagine alternative futures. This was accompanied by extensive online material such as zines and radio broadcasts, and it is worth noting that this project used more than 1 million pounds of its budget to create 800 commissions targeting 18- to 25-year-old artists most affected by the COVID-19 lockdowns. Overall the subject matter of the festival was decidedly future oriented apart from outlier *StoryTrails*, a project headed by David Olusoga focused on bringing minoritised histories to life through VR and AR technology. In its deployment of cutting-edge technology to explore aspects of the British past, *StoryTrails* perhaps most closely aligns with the FOB's focus on offering a narrative of the nation. Yet considering both festivals together more broadly across their temporal gap can help illuminate how current national crises have historically accumulated.

In order to analyse the FOB and Unboxed, I conceptually draw on Stuart Hall's applications of conjuncture as a method to read the contemporary moment. Lawrence Grossberg defines conjuncture as located between the specificity of the moment and the longue durée of the epoch (1981: 42). Such an approach is illuminated in Hall's own work on Thatcherism as well as in his collaborations, notably in his work with Bill Schwarz on the crisis in social democracy which I will elaborate on further. Taking this work as a starting point, my initial exploration attempts a similar linkage between the specificity of contemporary discourses and experiences of race and racialisation in the British context as they link back to the early moment of decolonisation in 1951, and through this empire. I also seek to foreground the operations of the state which while couched in discourses of nation in both 1951 and 2022 enact through legal and material means the conditions which make specific discourses of the nation cohere. However, in the process of writing this Element, other aspects of our current conjuncture started to insistently reveal themselves, most prominently the increased proliferation of catastrophes wrought by the climate crisis against a backdrop of the revived seduction of late fascist imaginaries

(Toscano, 2024). In stressing Cultural Studies' materialist groundings, Jeremy Gibert argues that conjunctural analysis 'does not prescribe in advance how much weight is to be given to "cultural", economic, political, social or technological factors in making an overall analysis of a given social formation or period' (2019: 10). The prominent role given to technology within both festivals, and its imbrication with economic and political structures of their distinct, yet interlinked, periods, increasingly led me to consider how my cultural analysis would need to be weighted against the factors identified by Gilbert. Thus the epoch-defining moment of empire exposed a set of ramifications which extended beyond straightforward readings of identity and social stratification, bringing the initial and continued role of capitalist exploitation, extraction and environmental degradation into sharp relief.

Conjunctural analysis thus helps reveal how the many lethal and painful connections of the present demand deeper excavations of historical processes that created and continue to shape them. This is evident not only in the case of the climate, but also in all manner of violences heaped up in the short period of writing this Element: livestreamed genocide, the renewed brutal enforcement of binary sex gender systems and an ascendant global fascism, to name a few. Alberto Toscano argues against analogical modes of defining the latter according to its twentieth-century European variants and considers instead fascism's mutable character, stretching here again from a deeper past and into later futures. Quoting Langston Hughes, W.E.B. Du Bois, Albert Memmi and Aimé Césaire, he draws attention to how modes of colonial governance as well as historical experiences of Black Americans already evidence a racial fascism that has gone unremarked, because it operates on the other side of the colour-line (28). He also notes current fascist imaginaries depart from their European predecessors in how they do not seek to appeal to some vague, romantic and often pre-capitalist other. Rather, Toscano argues that contemporary fascist projects

> are seemingly driven by *a nostalgia for synchronicity*, for the 'Fordist' heyday of Big Capital and Big Labour (generally coded as male and white) and for a certain ideology of modernisation. No archaic pasts or invented traditions here, but the hankering for the image of a moment ... for a racialised and gendered image of the patriotic industrial worker. (9)

This image is in no small ways reminiscent of aspects of the Festival of Britain I will discuss in this Element: lionised workers, modernisation and industry. I write this not to call the 1951 event or the period of its creation fascist – this would flatten out the appeal for the careful historical excavation I am trying to argue for. However, Toscano's assessment invites a question which I have attempted to consider in this Element. How might a closer scrutiny of this period, often remembered fondly for its progressive aspects, draw attention to the obfuscation of the violences necessary to maintain late capitalist modernity and its current morbid manifestation? Indeed, attending to the varying processes enabling these violences and their afterlives is but one pre-condition to resist and hopefully halt the disastrous trajectory facing many of us now, and in the not-so-distant future.

1.1 State Culture

Hopefully some of the similarities between both festivals have become clear. Both projects were driven by the intertwining of science with the arts, both emerged in moments of national change and both help illuminate the distinct historical conjunctures of their respective periods as well as how these inform each other across the seventy years separating them – especially with regard to empire, power and extraction. To a certain degree choosing to focus on two very well state-funded projects invested in forms of national pride may seem somewhat facile. However, such events also help to bring into relief certain aspects of culture's function within the apparatus of the liberal state. Despite some stark differences regarding the managing of resources and public services, in the first instance, the social-democratic state of 1951 and its 2022 Conservative successor were both predicated on the preservation of the capitalist economy. It is this shared feature which informs my decision to read both events through the lens of the state rather than the nation. As noted by the authors of Marxist Keywords for Performance: 'Domestically, the state stands above a nation of people that encounter each other as legally free and with equal rights to own and sell private property, including their own labour power ... A bourgeois state maintains the class relation, not just by suppressing proletarian resistance but also by regulating capital's most self-destructive tendencies' (Blackwell-Pal et al., 2021). While the state maintains the monopoly on the legitimate use of violence, its function is also to secure the social reproduction of its subjects in view of maintaining a capitalist economy, something it achieves through an acquiescence to its legitimacy. This acquiescence is partially produced through appealing to the concept of nation, which is in turn often articulated through the promotion of certain aspects of culture. The authors further argue that the proliferation of national cultural institutions and festivals which seek to foster a unified sense of identity buttress 'the similarly mediating concept of nation that seeks to overcome class antagonism through an appeal to the transcendent category of citizenship' (Blackwell-Pal et al., 2021). It is undeniable that both the FOB and Unboxed were specifically conceived as events to promote a sense of national pride as part of their brief: to be a 'tonic to the nation' in the case of the FOB and 'open, original and optimistic' in the case of Unboxed (DCMS, 2020) Moreover, while the FOB was most explicit in its desire to evoke a somewhat essentialised concept of citizenship grounded in a transhistorical and insular narration of British identity, Unboxed also evoked a certain bounded exceptionalism to Britishness.

Both events contained aspects of theatre and performance within their programming – although in neither case were these prominently centred. However, the festivals' theatrical dimension was also to be found in forms of interactive engagement as they ephemerally attempted to stage something like 'British identity' or 'British creativity' to consolidate a sense of collective belonging. As David Lloyd and Paul Thomas have argued, theatre presents as one of the most idealised metaphors for establishing the relationship between the state and culture in European liberal imaginaries. Through tracing the function of culture as a mode of shaping acquiescence to the liberal state across the late eighteenth and nineteenth centuries, they contend that the '"representations" that the theatre presents to the public replicate as normative narratives the very conditions that their assembly there enacts ... precisely because it is a recreationary space, its representations can never be more than prefigurative instances of an equality that is always yet to come' (1998: 57) Thus the theatrical apparatus becomes an exemplary model for thinking how the deployment of culture can both operate as and train people for the state's mediation of conflicts among interest groups. As Lloyd and Thomas argue 'it is the function of culture to interpellate individuals into the disposition to disinterested reflection that makes the state's mediations possible' (14). Culture, they assert 'produces the consensual ground for the state form of representative democracy by drawing the formal or representative disposition in every individual out of each person's concrete particularity' (14–15). This suggests a shared understanding of what this disinterested reflection amongst individuals might entail, perhaps through a harmonious recognition of one's citizenship. Through this, one's relationship to culture becomes unproblematically conceived of as desirable as spectators made citizens enter the institution which will allow them to watch a shared debate of common concern on equal footing. However, both festivals' relationship to questions of empire, power and, by extension, extraction complicates a straightforward reading of how both staged unified senses of identity, inviting a conjunctural analysis.

As argued by Toscano, Hall's conjunctural analysis of Thatcherism remains profoundly pertinent to our authoritarian moment in its diagnosis of how populism gestated in the 1960s and 1970s around a concatenation of moral panics and that in this sense 'racism was ... a kind of supplement to neoliberalism' (68). Paradigmatically in Hall's work these panics were linked to muggings but as

Toscano argues, over the years these have subsequently shifted to topics such as 'radical' Islam, transgender identity, knife crime or Eastern European migration. According to Hall such moral panics help ground 'neoliberal politics directly in an appeal to 'the people'; to root them in the essentialist categories of common sense and practical moralism – and this to construct, not simply awaken, classes, groups and interests into a particular definition of 'the people' (71). Hall and Bill Schwarz also situate this diagnosis of the political and economic crises of the late 1970s in a much longer history of unresolved antagonisms between state driven collectivism and both left wing and liberal challenges to it. They thus locate this crisis in the gradual ascendancy of Fabianist social-democracy between 1880s and the 1950s/60s, predicated as it was on a Gramscian 'passive revolution' that is a 'historical occasion in which a "revolution" was installed from above, in order to forestall a threat from below ... marking both an important reordering of state and civil society and a restoration of the fundamental social relations of production on a more stable basis for the future' (Hall and Schwarz, 2021: 114). Hall offers further considerations of this claim in his foundational essay on the success of Thatcherism, 'The Great Moving Right Show', which analyses the Conservative party's success in harnessing anti-state sentiment for right-wing reform. Here again he points to Labour's Fabian-collectivist inheritance, a gradualist, patrician and eventually reformist approach to implementing socialist redistributive principles via the obtention of state power. Hall notes how the 'expansion of the state machine ... has often been defined in its tradition as synonymous with socialism itself' and that 'Labour has been willing to use this state to reform conditions for the working people, provided it not bite too deeply into the "logic" of capitalist accumulation' (1981: 386). Hall and Schwarz also contend that the crisis of liberalism which occurred over Britain's long economic decline between the 1880s and the 1970s also leads to the 'crisis in social democracy' of the 1970s and 1980s, noting that 'even during the height of the consumer boom and 'consensus' politics of the 1950s this long term economic decline was not structurally reversed' (121). This long economic decline is in no small part linked to the decline of the British Empire, and as I will argue, the construction of a specifically insular British 'people'. Britain's imperial foundations and the consensual approach to managing class conflict and racial differences are thus not only fundamental in considering the FOB but also the context through which to read Unboxed festival.

1.2 Envisioning Consensus

This management of class conflict and racial difference is perhaps and easier object to critique in relationship to the FOB, often understood as the ruling

Labour governments' restructuring of the state to enable the historical compromise of social democracy. In his study of post-war London's large-scale urban restructuring, Hornsey encapsulates this investment best as he considers the festival's role in building consensus for political and economic transformation. Framing his critique of the festival through contemporaneous social democratic visions of urban planning imagined or enacted by the Labour government of the time, he notes that London planners sought to expunge postwar capitalism's most obvious forms of disharmony and believed that the

> reformed urban environment was the vehicle through which such tensions might be resolved, producing in its wake a more vibrant city in which the continuation of basic economic disparity would no longer be in conflict with the authorised performance of collective civic life. (10)

Hornsey's work offers some insightful insights into the performative disciplining of the movement of crowds on the FOB's exhibitions as one means of shaping such authorised performances of public life, underpinned by heteronormative understandings of social organisation.

This desire to expunge accounts of social disharmony in the festival's content is also noted in Conekin's foundational study of the festival, which alongside Hornsey's work informs my own writing on the FOB, *Autobiography of a Nation*. She similarly points to a consensual vison of social relations, prominently in the FOB's narrations of national histories. She writes: 'The role of the past in the 1951 Festival was to illustrate how the British people were unified, yet diverse, "cemented together" by character, tradition and ancient origins, no matter what their class tradition or geographical location' (82). These traditions were explored with various levels of detail across a wealth of mediums; in the larger urban exhibits and the travelling ones as well as in a series of thirteen distinct guides called 'About Britain', all offering distinct, yet linked, portraits of an insular people engaged in playful regional rivalries and eccentric traditions. This appears in stark contrast to the ongoing existence of the country's still vast imperial reach, and its recent granting of citizenship to Commonwealth subjects in 1948. These examples give an indication of how the festival situated Britain's internal differences and global position, perhaps most perfectly encapsulated in the poster for the Exhibition of science (see Figure 1).

Encircled by an atom, a design characteristic of the FOB, we see planet earth positioned in space, with an enormous Britain and island of Ireland seemingly taking up half of the world's surface, with no other land or continents around them. Shining outwards towards adjacent constellations, the picture suggests both a monumental vision of Britain's global and cosmic centrality and a deeply entrenched insularity in which the country and its adjacent colony radiate

Figure 1 Robin Day, poster for the Exhibition of Science (1951). Courtesy Robin & Lucienne Day Foundation/V&A Archive

individual achievement. Hornsey reads this as an image of security, making Britain 'appear lasting and secure' and an 'imagining of how historical change could be kept at bay', an analysis he also applies to the Skylon, a structure indicating the 'emptying of the historical future' (77; 61). These understandings do map neatly onto aspects of a social democratic vision rid of class conflict. Yet more can be written about how the poster entrenches a mythology of a nation entirely disconnected from any significant European or Global relationships. More blatantly perhaps, how Britain's centrality becomes visualised in the poster is predicated on exactly the extractive colonial relationships that were to be muted at the event itself. As Jo Littler has argued in her analysis of evocations of the Commonwealth in the festival: 'At a moment when Britain was relying more rather than less on trading within the empire, the Commonwealth's wealth was not so much held in common as being commonly channelled to Britain' (2006: 30).

The main South Bank exhibition avoided any explicit engagement with imperial relationships as they stood in 1951. Yet the place of 'The Commonwealth', as it was starting to be referred to more frequently since the 1926 Balfour declaration, remained unavoidable in the discussions of national success and national identity (Littler, 2006). Here other aspects of the festival betray how central conversations on the representations of empire and the Commonwealth were in the run-up to the festival and the festival itself. The only explicit event showcasing Empire was the 'Traditional Art from the Colonies' exhibition which happened in the imperial institute in Kensington after some debate. In reaching its final decision on what would constitute an appropriate display, the subcommittee on Commonwealth involvement notes that 'that the scope of the exhibition be limited to authentic traditional art and craftwork, and that modern developments affected by European influence, such as recently established schools of painting, should be excluded or treated as a distinct section' (FOB Committee Minutes November, 1949). Removing European aesthetic influences thus serves to obscure the cultural impact of colonialisation while maintaining their supposed mastery. As Conekin argues, viewers were constructed as part of a 'white we' unified in their comprehension that colonised people 'were not irredeemably inferior, they were "poetic" because they lacked the advantages that the scientific revolution had offered Europeans' (195). However, traces of Britain's imperial relationships were also to be found throughout the main exhibits as some festival committee minutes pertaining to Commonwealth attest:

> Instead of singling out for demonstration our part in colonising one part of the Empire, the Secretary of State felt that our contribution to world development and the achievement of independence in the United States and the Dominions, drawing attention to our contribution in the form of legal system, language, Parliamentary system, etc., might well be demonstrated in an exhibition. (1949)

This oblique assessment of the benefits of empire were often presented in the most benign terms, such as the following assessment of a supposed British inclination towards sporting games and their roles as great 'codifiers of sport' in their ability to 'adapt other people's games' (South Bank Catalogue: 79).

The most revealing of these assessments are to be found in the section regarding the Dome of Discovery's Sea and Ships section, where in assessing Britain's greatness as a seafaring nation, the catalogue states: 'Without the enterprise of our ship owners and their associates in the vast business operating shipping lines, the growth of the British Commonwealth could have followed very different trends' (36–37). I will return to this specific evocation of history in its replication aboard the Sea Travelling Exhibition. However, I hope that at this stage the relationship between Britain and its colonies is finally, if inadvertently, made clear. The insularity and scale of the nation suggested in the exhibition of science poster is inextricably tied to maritime trade routes themselves both producing the Commonwealth and consuming its spoils without which the people of this otherwise doggedly insular nation would starve, even as it wants to reach outer space. The Skylon offers perhaps an even clearer metaphor of this relationship. Hornsey's assessment of the structure is grounded in a comparison with Nelson's column, stressing the ahistorical impulse at the heart of its concept. He contends that 'while Nelson's column could still ask questions about a dynamic history of colonial expansion, the Skylon merely posed the riddle of how it could stay up. As a monument to the future, it was sorely undermined by its lack of vison about the possibility of social change' (61). Hornsey's comparison to Nelson's column is productive and points to the broader social democratic context of the festival grounded in a top-down attempt to quell class antagonism. Yet in contrasting the Skylon to an earlier monument squarely indicative of Britain's imperial exploits he also points to another way in which this arrest of history occurs, namely the erasure of the very material ways in which Britain's new social democratic economy did stand up: imperial conquest and extraction. This omission, I will argue, also perdures into Unboxed's twenty-first-century offerings. While most of Britain's former imperial territories have achieved formal decolonisation, empire's consequences remain a structuring facet of today's contemporary global conjuncture, notably in relationship to practices of bordering, agri-business and the ever-worsening climate crisis.

1.3 Mutable Differences

In contrast to 1951 Britain it would be difficult to present the country as an all-white nation. Despite the lingering of post-imperial nostalgia, it would be unfair to claim that no discursive reckoning with empire has happened, even as demands to uncover links to imperial plunder are increasingly framed through the framework of a culture war. When surveying the ten projects of Unboxed itself, efforts towards racial and other diversities are evident, most prominently in *StoryTrails* which in conversation with the Lion and Unicorn Pavilion underpins my exploration of migration and racialisation within a British social context. *StoryTrails* was the only project grappling with specific minoritised histories. However, the teams across all ten events all made concerted efforts to be inclusive of forms of ethnic, gender and sexual diversity, and none outwardly championed British exceptionalism. *Our Place in Space*, for example, stressed the country's insignificance when considered on cosmic scale in a near-inversion of the exhibition of science poster – albeit from a Northern Irish position which quite consciously drew on the territory's ongoing conflict as a starting point for this claim. As previously stated, Unboxed's overarching brief was to be 'open, original and optimistic', yet an unease about the festival's Brexit links persisted. For Martin Green the fault lies in the expressed ideological conflicts surrounding the festival. 'Rule one of major events: don't politicise them. And unfortunately a few chose to politicise it from the beginning' (McGurk, 2022). Yet, as with the FOB's own contested conception as simply a showcase for Labour's social democratic achievements, it is impossible to not consider how this generously funded project of national celebration might function with regard to the ruling Conservative government of 2022 and more broadly the contemporary operations of the British sate. While the misnomer 'Festival of Brexit' does overstate this specific orientation of Conservative politics in the final delivery of Unboxed, its focus on both internal diversity and technology formally and thematically does link it back to the FOB. As a similar attempt to represent something of the country to itself, the relationship between culture and the British state must similarly be considered.

Here again Hall offers some illuminating reflections regarding the 'multicultural question' which came to be prominent in understanding the managing of racial diversity by the British state from the mid 1960s onwards, defined by the racialised 'tightening of *external* immigration controls was the imposition of an increasingly potent *internal* race relations regime' (Ashcroft and Bevir, 2018: 5). While expressing cautious hope that multiculturalism might hold some possibility for reconfiguring social relations Hall points to the limits of the market-liberal multicultural project underpinning the New Labour government's approach to diversity at the turn of the century. Hall writes that

> we cannot simply reaffirm individual liberty and formal equality (what New Labour disarmingly calls 'equality of worth') because we can see both their inadequacy to the complexities of attachment, belongingness, and identity which multicultural society introduces, and the deep injustices of inequality, social exclusion, and injustice which continue to be perpetrated in their name. (2000: 125)

He considers the 'haphazard responses' in aspects of certain cultural practices through certain legal affordances (the wearing of turbans, consensual arranged marriages) against an erosion of the commitment to the welfare state, and also notes the temporal proximity between the fiftieth anniversary of the arrival of the *Empire Windrush* and the delayed McPherson report's conclusion that institutional racism played a role in the 1993 killing of by Stephen Lawrence by white supremacists (119; 126). With some foresight, he warns that what presents as a propitious moment for the multicultural question as it is emerging from below is always also a moment of danger, giving rise to new exclusionary binaries of cultural difference in the form of renewed far-right attempts to reconfigure homogenous understandings of British identity (126).

Sita Balani additionally draws attention to how a new 'flexible, market-oriented, innovative, entrepreneurial, and self-governing subject – an empowered individual – underpinned the forms of racial differentiation fortified by New Labour' (2023: 83). She argues that discourses of sexual modernity were a cornerstone of these new modes of racial stratification and discipline, alongside the myth of meritocracy. Under New Labour, Muslims, for example, became increasingly demonised for perceived forms of sexual backwardness produced by excessive community bonds, against the backdrop of the War on Terror. Meanwhile, Balani argues that

> the assimilation of upwardly mobile Indians fractured the category of British Asian but fortified the system of racial governance using a logic that would be finessed by subsequent Tory governments in the twenty-first century. Further, this image of the upwardly mobile, successful, aspirational Indian acted as evidence of the meritocracy New Labour claimed to promote. (98)

Thus, at 'the start of the 2020s, there were more black and brown faces among the political elite than ever before'. This elite's actions fully embrace new exclusionary logics of cultural difference diagnosed by Hall in 2000 – be it Priti Patel and Suella Braverman's unashamed embrace of militarised, violent and outsourced border regimes, Kemi Badenoch's attacks on critical race theory or Savid Javid tweeting about 'sick Asian paedophiles' (99–100). While Hall in 2000 shows some modicum of hope that select aspects of multiculturalism might deepen democratic practices in social life, Balani establishes that meritocratic market-liberalism simply allowed some upwardly mobile and/or generationally wealthy grandchildren of the colonies to successfully participate in xenophobic constructions of the British nation (125). The cosmetic representation of difference at certain levels of power thus simply serves to maintain the lethal exclusionary logics of the British state elsewhere. In turn, the embrace of these exclusionary logics by racialised, yet empowered, individuals at the helm of government enables any discussions of racism to appear as nothing but a conspiracy theory (Balani: 138).

Central to the making of race over the last century looms the border. Insofar as the ahistorical construction of Britain as a self-contained island nation with a shared culture starts fully solidifying over the large-scale decolonisation of the 1960s, it is in large parts the expansion of legal technologies of bordering occurring alongside the shrinking of Empire that materially intervene in the composition of national identity. These changes in migration and asylum law will be the focus of my first section. I will consider how evocations of Britain as a historically and racially homogenous nation in 1951 lays the ground for subsequent arguments for increasingly harsh migration laws predicated on the myth of Britain as a bounded territorial entity, despite the incorporation of the 1948 'Windrush generation' into the British state, and its subsequent cultural representations as evidenced in Unboxed's *Stoytrails*. The FOB's Lion and Unicorn Pavilion offers a productive example of how social-democratic understandings of distinct British traditions occlude both Empire and post Norman migratory influxes to the country. Such a conception thus lays the ground for an increased bordered hermeticism, even as understandings of Britishness appear somewhat more elastic in the face of 2022's transformed racial fabric. While discourses of internal diversities already present in 1951 enable a widened understanding of who might be counted as an authentic Briton within 2022's national boundaries, I will argue that the relationship between the border and race inflected by the longer impact of Empire continues to structure the country's internal racial ordering.

I will then turn to the representations of extractive practices in my second section and consider the role of coal and oil in contributing to both British historical supremacy in the form of industrial development and its consequences in the form of climate change and corporatisation. I will compare the Industrial Power Exhibition held in Glasgow as part of the FOB with *Seemonster*, an oil rig repurposed as an energetically self-sustaining installation in the English seaside town of Weston-super-Mare. Thus, I will trace how both projects serve to obfuscate aspects of extraction in a wish to conjure either heroic or comforting understandings of British identity, notably in how they approach the question of work and workers. The IPE's deployment of miners demonstrating their craft and use of new technologies can be located in contemporaneous heroic representations of miners as the backbone of the post-war reconstruction effort. *Seemonster* conversely presented visitors with an image of green energy production devoid of any representation or discussion of offshore labour whatsoever, extending the installation's self-sustainability to the conceptualisation of Britain itself. Drawing on Shane Boyle theorisations of the use of drones in art, I will also argue that *Seemonster*'s technological displays, in erasing the labour necessary to extraction might in fact help draw attention to the exploitative and continued need for human workers.

My final section will return to questions of imperial conquest, focusing on extraction and its contemporary consequences. I will first explore how

Britain's naval proficiency is narrated aboard the temporarily decommissioned military vessel HMS *Campania* for its Sea Travelling Exhibition, intimately intertwined the country's scientific progress with the development of Commonwealth territories. This will offer a point of departure for exploring Britain's first nuclear tests conducted in its former Australian colony in 1952, with the HMS *Campania* as its flag bearer, in stark opposition to discussions of atomic power throughout the festival. I will also turn to appropriation of land and agricultural development as a logic of colonial and capitalist development. Linking this to Ellen Meiksins Wood's work on the rural origins of capitalism will help me expand my analysis towards the recent reckoning with the global COVID-19 pandemic. The pandemic was an implicit formal and thematic feature of Unboxed's show *About Us*, couched within a larger preoccupation with planetary life and human technology. The show was framed through the overarching visual motif of the network, projected in various guises onto the facades of historical buildings throughout the country and choral evocations of togetherness. I will thus link Lockean seventeenth-century theories and practices of agricultural improvement to the development mid-century agri-business all the way to their consequences role in the evolution of ever new viruses. In turn this will lead me to critique how the temporally and spatially flattening motif of the network obscures certain origins of our current crises and weakens capacity for social change through its denial of history.

Overall, my twinning of both events across time will move from an assessment of empire's afterlives in the lived realities of racial stratification in contemporary Britain to its enduring effects in the shape of extraction and ecological degradation. Approaching these questions through a conjunctural analysis, I seek to highlight imperial Britain's central role in the origins of our current crises, especially when understood alongside the gradual establishment of a global capitalist economy. As Andreas Malm notes: 'Only by seeing the British imperialists as agents on a very, very special mission ... can we understand the causes and import of their actions. Nature did not impel them to search for coal; society did not set up the atmosphere. The fallout materialised at the intersection' (47). While both festivals' shape lend themselves to forms of spatial reading which can allow for immediate apprehensions of presences and absences in their respective contemporary time, following Malm and Hall I seek to layer my argument with deeper historical and material excavations which focus as much on the longue durée as they do on what is instantly available to the viewer – starting with the intimate intertwining of empire, British identity and the continual expansion of migration law between 1951 and 2022.

2 Bordered Identities

In his essay accompanying Steve McQueen's 2023 film *Grenfell*, a meditation on the 2017 West London tower block fire in which seventy-two people lost their lives screened at the Serpentine Gallery in 2023, Paul Gilroy remarks that 'the true horror of these killings is that they present in capsule form a deeply disturbing illustration of the morbidity of institutions in contemporary Britain' (8). Comparing the responses to this event to the 1981 New Cross fire, a presumed act of arson by neo-Nazis in which thirteen young Black people celebrating a birthday lost their lives, he continues:

> The resulting violence is both fast and slow ... Ordinary working people, considered superfluous or unwanted, are exiled to a grey zone where justice cannot enter and their less-than-worthy lives count for next to nothing. Those denizens do not belong in this area. The lives of the lowly are inconsequential. From on high, they may even appear as waste in human shape. (9)

Of all the ordinary working people who lost their lives in the fire, 57 (85 per cent) were from minority ethnic backgrounds, and of the further white victims, many were EU migrants. Many articles and discussions of Grenfell's aftermath ask us to consider its 'longs shadow' – all the consequences wrought by the catastrophe in terms of post-traumatic stress disorder, housing insecurity, long-term health impacts and glaring racial inequalities – 40 per cent of high-rise inhabitants, for example, are from Black, Arab or Asian communities when they represent 14 per cent of the population (Maragh et al., 2020). Insofar as Grenfell crystallises the racist inequalities which continue to characterise contemporary Britain, its shadow stretches long into the past as much as it does the present and future. Indeed, as Nadine El-Enany has argued, it is vital to be attentive to Britain's colonial configuration and its legacy of racism as a factor in what made the victims of the fire (2019: 83). El-Enany draws attention the afterlives of imperial management systems as these have transformed to adapt to Britain's national territory after the gradual loss of empire, not least through practices of population management, and crucially bordering.

The relationship between bordering, race and understandings of British identity is the focus of this section. First, I explore how the Festival of Britain's evocation of a national identity can be seen as a precursor for subsequent discursive and legal frameworks giving this identity an insular and increasingly hermetic character, while also counterintuitively paving the way for forms of internal difference. Such understandings would eventually enable understandings of race as an individual marker increasingly uncoupled from its enduring imperial histories, despite the evident persistence of these histories' afterlives in the ongoing effects of institutional racism of which Grenfell offers a particularly brutal example. This context enables me to consider how this uncoupling might operate in the present day in an analysis of Unboxed's *StoryTrails* AR-enhanced audio walks. The urban backdrops of *StoryTrails*' London locations – Brixton and Catford – are decisive in my interpretation, particularly as these similarly conjure the grey zones evoked by Gilroy in their differentiated management of local, ordinary and overwhelmingly racialised people.

2.1 Identity at the Festival: Traditionally Modern

Hall's noted 'long-term economic' decline and concomitant construction of a specifically insular British people inform this section alongside shifts in migratory policies that accompanied these changes. Fundamental to this long-term economic decline, as already noted, is Britain's progressively weakening position as the world's largest empire. Yet despite the loss of most of Ireland in 1922 and the independence and subsequent partition of India and Pakistan in 1947, followed by Sri Lanka and Myanmar in 1948, the Attlee government was not in any way committed to overseeing further decolonisation, even as a reward for colonial subjects loyally fighting on Britain's side during the Second World War. As argued by Charlotte Lydia Riley, it was predicted that some African colonies would attain independence only by the end of the century and that despite 'the rise of independence movements in many areas of the empire, British colonial policy operated as if the continued integrity of the empire was a given, at least for the foreseeable future' (2024: 53). Furthermore, Riley notes that for some Britons the Attlee government enabled increased exposure to empire and imperial peoples, be it via the 1949 Colonial Exhibition or the mythologised 1948 arrival of the *Empire Windrush*, or indeed the *Art from the Colonies* exhibition held as part of the FOB. Yet the festival arguably foreshadows the gradual construction of a more bounded national mindset. Mentions of imperial might were explicitly muted, morphing instead into celebrations of the Commonwealth, which, although not unproblematic, tended to focus on ideas of cultural exchange between people rather than fully championing Britain's supposed benevolent rule over her colonial children. More importantly, however, the primary focus of the festival was resolutely on the people of the island of Britain and its attendant Northern Irish colony, as narrations of identity focused in on differences within these territories.

In her extensive work on the festival, Becky Conekin notes that the festival's predominant imaginings of the British people were those embedded in 'universal time', imagined as transhistorical and trans-class. She remarks that:

> The official festival's understanding of who was British is clear – those people whose ancestors came here as Normans, Saxons, Iron Age Celts,

Romans, Vikings, or as Stone Age 'colonists.' ... This conception of Britishness, as reaching back to the Normans and before, clearly excluded Black British subjects, as well as the most significant groups of people to immigrate to Britain before the late 1940s: the Irish and the Jews from many nations for generations. (101)

This positioning of British identity as becoming historically defined around the moment of what would be evoked by radical movements and histories (of all stripes) as the Norman Yoke may appear curious; it had already been three years since the arrival of the HMS *Empire Windrush* at Tilbury Docks on the 22 June 1948. Although not technically the first post-war ship carrying migrants from the Caribbean, nor in fact a boat only carrying people from the West Indies, the docking of the *Empire Windrush* has nevertheless come to emblematically represent the post-war Black migrant experience (Riley: 61–62). Thus, in their effort to detach British identity from any imperial connections, the organisers of the festival recast Britishness along very narrow ethno-nationalist lines which would see it solidified in the eleventh century. Yet, somewhat counterintuitively, internal diversities were also recurrently stressed. Conekin remarks that the Sea Travelling exhibition's catalogue describes the British as a much mixed race while the guide to the People of Britain Pavilion states that they are certainly one of the most mixed people in the world, and asks: 'What different breeds of ancestors have contributed to such a rare miscellany of faces as confronts the visitor in any London bus?' (63) While in the context of 1951 Britain, this diversity's origin was anchored around a millennia ago, this framing of a national fabric grounded in internal diversity did echo and expand across time without fundamentally unsettling aspects of the country's racial ordering.

Conekin locates a prominent example of such an imagining in the Lion and Unicorn Pavilion, an exhibit displaying British character and tradition, described in the catalogue as follows: '"The Lion and the Unicorn" – serves to symbolise two of the main qualities of the national character: on one hand, realism and strength, on the other fantasy, independence and imagination.' The pavilion itself is an airy and light structure, with a curved roof and a panelled glass front and side wall, reminiscent of the Royal Festival Hall in style and described by Katherine Howells as a 'picture of modern simplicity' (Howells, 2021). This assessment is confirmed in her interview with Henrietta Goodden, daughter of the pavilion's architect, Robert Goodden: 'There was a light-heartedness about it which I think is the thing that comes through really. It was all about airiness and being uplifting; about colour and space. Everything was very bleak after the war and the whole of the Southbank was all about lifting the national character' (Howells, 2021). Inside, the modern design mingles with displays of arts and crafts, creating a relatively idiosyncratic visual interpretation of British identity blending progressive traditions, crafts, artistic interpretations of the themes of the pavilion and some cutting-edge interactive technology. White plastic doves hang from its ceiling, escaping a large wicker cage hung high above the entrance, adding a sense of whimsy to the light and modernist environment of the pavilion's structure.

After being greeted by their first model of a Lion and Unicorn, visitors are first directed to the upstairs gallery focusing on the 'English Language', followed by 'Eccentricity and Humour', 'Skill', 'British Freedoms' and finally 'Nature'. The lion and unicorn remain a motif throughout the visitors' journey. Opening the English language section the beasts are found balancing on ladders holding up a world map with the heading 'English is a World language' and subtitled with 'English is understood almost everywhere ... and the English almost nowhere' (FOB: 1951). The world's (unexplained) global reach of English is also supplemented by the global popularity of English literature, exemplified by the display of forty different Shakespeare translations and some accompanying miniature model sets. In contrast, the most futuristic element of the whole pavilion is also presented here, an interactive screen which viewers can use to listen to local accents and dialects, which according to Goodden present the 'remarkable diversity of nation's tongue: every county in the British Isles contributed a locally-used idiom or phrase' (2011: 99). Before descending back below, visitors are faced with the *Country Life* mural by Edward Bawden, taking up the whole back wall of the pavilion crinkled into vertical facets 'like a partly open fan', depicting vignettes of rural life: fragments of villages, seaside landscapes, and, notably, agriculture and mining – a key theme across the festival to be explored in more detail in subsequent sections (Goodden and Russell, 1976: 98). Visitors then descend the mezzanine and invited to explore the FOB's interpretation of British eccentricity and humour – most prominently represented by a large statue of *Alice through the Looking Glass*' white knight. Here visitors can also enjoy a range of eccentric inventions and novelties such as miniature tea sets. Finally again two smaller sections which, under the terms 'skill' and 'nature', focus primarily on craft – an indication of the designers and architects' interest in the art and crafts movement (see Figure 2). The last section of the pavilion on the way to the exit, it showcases a range of native British plants as well as artefacts and household objects inspired by the British natural world, placed on shelves against the glass side wall of the pavilion. While each of these sections offers some noteworthy constructions of Britishness, especially in the interlinking of craft and nature, it is the Freedom section, alongside the exploration of the English language, that remains the

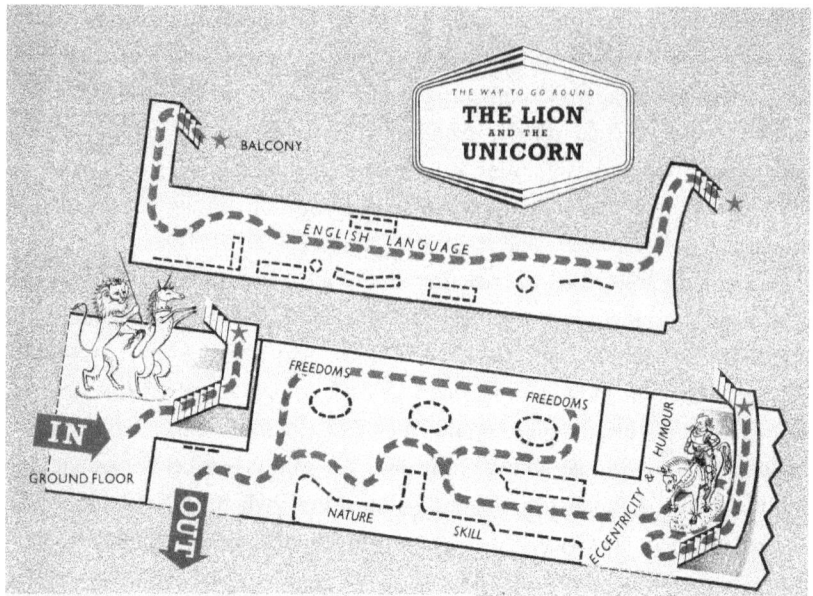

Figure 2 Lion and the Unicorn. Guide to South Bank Exhibition, London. Festival of Britain (1951). Curtesy of the National Archives, Kew.

most explicit in how British people might be invited to think about the specificity of their national identity.

A relatively sparse space, visitors first encounter a large slab of grey engraved stone on their right, bearing these words by poet and former international brigades volunteer Laurie Lee: 'British freedom is made from rough beginnings. It is based on the freedom of worship, of government, and of the person. Much sweat went to shape it, much blood to protect it. Its pattern now familiar across the world' (FOB, 1951). Three freestanding 'monuments' stand across from this engraving and parallel to a mural on the adjoining wall: a life-size Celtic cross, a High Court judge's robe and wig surrounded by legal tomes and finally the Union flag surrounded by its contributory crosses of St George, St Patrick and St Andrew, honouring in turn Christianity, Law and the Constitution (Goodden and Russell, 1976: 98). The centrepiece of this section spanning most of the wall is another mural created by Kenneth Rowntree named *The Freedoms*, depicting a series of historical events presented as intrinsic to British liberty: the Magna Carta, freedom of the press, women's right to vote, Catholics' right to worship and the Tolpuddle martyrs. As if to counteract Lee's lofty definition of British freedom, Rowntree's style is colourful and simple in his depictions which are presented as vignettes in chronological order from left to right, ending with the independence of India and Pakistan. As is stressed in the catalogues, these historical depictions illustrate how the British have, throughout their history, 'probed for the weak spot of enemies for their freedom and always swiftly broken through' (1951: 68). According to Conekin, these specific versions of British liberty are heavily inflected by Labour, especially in its evocation of the Tolpuddle Martyrs which in 1951 would still have stood as a fragile and invented national tradition (98).

For all the celebration of popular struggles, at this juncture there is evidence of a glaring silence – namely, the role of empire in the spread of the English language and the freedoms of colonial subjects the British might have themselves suppressed, some just recently made British in status if not in the imaginary of a bounded Britain. This purposeful omission has been noted extensively in scholarship on the festival, prominently Conekin who dedicates a whole chapter to this appropriately named 'The place that was almost absent: the British Empire' (2003). Howells and Gooden, whose assessments are arguably more celebratory, also note this gap. Jo Littler usefully diagnoses the complimentary discourses on Empire across the FOB which oscillated between imperial mastery (in its depictions of scientific achievements), benevolent partnership (in its depictions of Commonwealth relationships and progress) and national parochialism, of which the Lion and Unicorn Pavilion is one of the most noteworthy examples (2006). Indeed, although the pavilion appears to depict the only explicit mention of colonisation in Rowntree's portrayal of Indian and Pakistan's independence, these are folded into a specifically British conceptualisation of freedom – and with no mention of the disastrous effects of the 1947 partition for both countries.

The parochial nature of the whimsical and seemingly diminished, inward-looking Britain evoked in the pavilion may now appear comical, but also surprising seeing the large swathes of the planet then still technically ruled by Britain. Yet, as noted by Kojo Koram, some of the background noise to the creation of the welfare state was the need for a new nationalism in the face of Britain's crumbling empire, noting that the Labour Party's 1945 election manifesto contains 'the word "health" nine times, "social" is mentioned sixteen times but the "nation" is raised twenty-seven times' (89–90).

Koram thus argues that the spirit of forty-five became a key tool in the erasure of empire, tying the victory of 1945 to the new welfare state and ensuring that in popular memory the 1950s and 1960s would be remembered for the development of social democracy rather than decolonisation (90). Britain needed to define an overarching idea of national character underpinned by a contained version of shared history and crucially of a nationally united, if 'diverse' people – as indicated most strikingly in the exhibition by the recordings of local idioms. Insofar as Hall is incisive in diagnosing Thatcherism's harnessing of a certain idea of 'the people' for the development of her authoritarian form of populism, the FOB's evocations of a certain British psyche – which at times simply slips into Englishness – demonstrates how some groundwork was already laid out by a Labour government eager to maintain popular consensus.

The juxtaposition of temporalities between the modern architectural style, contemporary renderings of historical struggles and evocations of a people whose ethnic identity is evoked as fully stable since the eleventh century offers a direct example of Koram's assessment of Labour's overall project. This juxtaposition is also noted by Conekin as she considers how the interactive idiomatic recordings, sitting next to Shakespeare and an Oxford Lectern Bible, work to link the present to a very long sense of the past (96). Without disregarding the struggles for labour rights and equality depicted on the mural, the pavilion offers an example of what might retroactively be read as progressive patriotism, a discursive move that celebrates native struggles against power and offers promises of socialism within the strict boundaries of the nation itself. As argued by the authors of *Empire's Endgame*, progressive patriotism is an essentially aphasic operation, noting that the 'allure of progressive patriotism therefore relies on a set of assumptions about the value of differently racialised people; foreigners are placed outside of progressive narratives of a nation supposedly grounded in working-class solidarity' (63). Aphasia is certainly at play in the whole of the FOB, with all its joyous narrations of a benevolent Commonwealth drawing viewers' attention away from the actual geopolitical realities of 1951, although, as I will argue later, never far from fully revealing empire's enduring effects. Rather, the reconfiguration of the British state through both a discourse of nation and one of radical struggle against oppression performs a double move through which Britain becomes bounded and increasingly bordered all the while claiming that this bounded and bordered identity is innately inflected by a desire for justice. More perversely perhaps, such modes of apprehending a form of British exceptionalism continue to carry through history and are malleable enough to be reconfigured for both liberal and reactionary projects. Claims that quirky internal differences are a form of national characteristic alongside an innate desire for justice enable these two alleged qualities of Britishness to be rearranged in later decades without fundamentally impacting either Britain's relationship to empire, or its bordered boundedness.

2.2 Post-War Migrations: Celebrations and Scandals

How did these shifts in British identity occur between 1948 and 2022? Key to these transformations is legislation – beginning with the 1948 British

Nationality Act which brought the *Empire Windrush* to Tilbury Docks. Indeed, the Commonwealth migration which arrived in Britain after its passing is now colloquially described as 'the Windrush generation'. El-Enany traces the initial decision to give forty-eight territories falling under the category of 'United Kingdom and colonies' an unqualified right to enter and remain in the United Kingdom as a reaction to Canada's introduction of its own citizenship law which demoted British subjecthood through stipulating that the latter now derived from Canadian citizenship (77–78). This created a fear that the Old (settler) Dominions would abandon their subordinate association with Britain and that creating a further category of subjects without citizenship could demonstrate that 'the position of white British settlers was of the utmost importance' (79). According to El-Enany and contrary to popular belief, the Act's purpose was not about encouraging immigration of specific subjects to Britain to aid post-war reconstruction but simply 'deemed necessary to maintain the Empire' (79). Indeed she notes that the possibility that 'racialised colony and Commonwealth citizens would travel to and live in Britain was not contemplated in Parliament' (80). While some recruitment schemes did target racialised colonial and Commonwealth citizens, most were geared towards other white Europeans such as Poles. British mainland officials in fact warned West Indian governors that encouraging the migration of Black British subjects might lead to the introduction of controls.

Thus, the attempt in the Lion and Unicorn Pavilion and the festival more broadly to entrench an insular British identity composed of internal diversities developed between a people stretching back to the Normans while holding the empire, Commonwealth and contemporary migratory flows at arm's length is noteworthy. The political contradictions at the heart of the 1948 Act and subsequent efforts to mitigate its consequences are prefigured in the parochial ways British identity is narrated in the festival. In its attempt to fix British culture and identity – certainly as white but also specifically distinct from its recent imperial conception – the festival appears to prefigure some of the ongoing afterlives of these contradictions in current enactments of much harder xeno-racist policies. As the first modern national festival focused solely on the people of Britain and the six remaining colonised counties of the North of Ireland, and happening in near-conjunction with this immigration act, 1951 can be considered as a turning point of sorts. It inaugurated and entrenched at the level of national culture a blueprint for fixing British identity, even if this identity remains counter-intuitively malleable well into the twenty-first century, as will soon become evident. Craig Gilmore and Ruthie Wilson-Gilmore diagnose the state's management of racial categories as analogous to the management of infrastructure that needs to be periodically modernised. They further note that sometimes this results in 'protecting' certain racial groups, and other times in sacrificing them. (2007: 145). It is easy to map the British state's material racist management practices in the expansion of its immigration policies over the past seventy years alongside the selective protection or even lionising of certain racial groups in order to do so. Indeed, Britain's racial make-up is now much more evidently diverse that some of the poster children for extreme anti-immigration measures are themselves racialised as first- or second-generation children of migrant parents, as touched upon in the introduction. While on the surface, Britain's racial diversity is now understood as partially originating outside of the island itself, and formed by some of its formerly colonised subjects, an insular exceptionalism remains – one that has moved towards bordering technologies and internal modes of racial ordering, under the veneer of what the authors of empire's Endgame name 'representative anti-racism'.

This brings me to 2022, to consider how *StoryTrails*, a contemporary creative exploration of British identity at Unboxed Festival sits within its immediate context and in light of its 1951 predecessor. Out of the ten projects, *StoryTrails* was the most explicit showcase of British identities and histories. The project offered Virtual Reality (VR) experiences and Augmented Reality (AR) enhanced walks in select locations across the UK, exploring local stories and figures drawing on a selection of local and national archives. This project's executive producer was Professor of Black History David Olusoga OBE, notable for his accessible disseminations of Black British histories usually through the means of BBC TV documentaries. A prominent example of his work is his collaboration with University College London's Centre for the Study of the Legacies of British Slavery, led by Nicholas Draper and Catherine Hall to create a documentary using the centre's research on the compensation of slave owners after Britain's abolition of slavery in 1833 (Crichton, 2015). Olusoga's work overall has showcased the long-standing presence and contribution of Black people to Britain, from their presence at the Elizabethan court through to fighting in the First World War and the post-Windrush cultural assimilation of aspects of Black culture. The focus of *StoryTrails* was similarly on exploring hidden and minoritarian lives, with a strong focus on racialised people but also queer and working class as well women's stories. The project travelled to fifteen different locations, with its bases in local libraries where participants could pick up VR headsets to engage in a novel experience of their local environment.

Olusoga describes the impetus of the project as follows:

> The idea behind *StoryTrails* is that our 50 creatives will use the new technologies to help their communities reconnect to public spaces across the UK.

> They will do this by reanimating forgotten moments from our history, using the 3D internet to stamp that history virtually on to the places where it occurred. Windrush Square in Brixton will be occupied by the digital voices of people such as Olive Morris, a pioneer in the fight for racial equality back in the 1970s. (2022)

Locations were in part chosen due to their diminished access to both arts and culture and digital skills training infrastructures – upskilling local creative workers in the use of AR and VR technology was stressed in assessments of the projects' impact (The Best in Heritage, 2024). The project was led by Story Futures, a research and development programme based at Royal Holloway, University of London focused on 'placing innovative storytelling at the heart of the next generation of immersive technologies and experiences' (Story Futures). However, each city's specific stories were developed by local team members, tasked to uncover and map lesser-known figures and narratives surrounding their hometowns. The focus of these walks indicates a shared concern with the Lion and Unicorn pavilion's exploration of British identity as expressed in its history, even as these histories become more localised and specific rather than folded into a larger narrative of a universal British character. While I participated in many of these experiences remotely, my focus will be on the two South London locations for the walks: Lewisham and Lambeth. While I missed the full VR experience, I was in this case able to experience the augmented reality app-powered walks based in London.

The Lambeth trail departed from Windrush Square and invites me to become a roadie for Winifred (Winnie) Atwell, the first Black woman to achieve a number one single in the British charts in 1954. The trail, named *Winnie's Honky Tonk Walk*, takes me from the square around to Effra Road to learn about Winnie's debut playing ragtime in London while completing her training in classical music at the Royal Academy of Music upon her arrival to England in 1946. I then slowly make my way up Atlantic Road to visit the former location of the hair salon she opened after encountering success, which burnt down in the Brixton uprisings of 1981. I also hear about her difficulty breaking though in the United States due to racial segregation laws in force in the Southern states which cost her an appearance on the *Ed Sullivan Show*, impeding her transatlantic success. As the trail ends by the Lambeth Tate Library, back on Windrush square, I learn of her departure for a life in Australia. The AR elements offer three dimensional environments which map onto the surrounding environment of each walk and I am invited to tap and explore these elements, which display snippets of film archives and recorded material offering glimpses into aspects of either Winnie's life or more general contexts. The three-dimensional objects vary across the various stops, but are presented in period style, most prominently vintage mid-century furniture, radios and TV sets. The Lewisham walk begins underneath the large Catford Cat statue welcoming visitors into the 1974 Catford Centre Brutalist shopping complex. Our guide, a smaller blue cat jumps down. She seems confused about her origins, and I am tasked to help her discover these: the trail itself is named *New Cat in Town*. The itinerary similarly loops back around the streets surrounding the shopping centre to end in the local library in the centre itself. I am first taken into a virtual representation of a Vietnamese restaurant to explore food and witness my small guide's curiosity for a large bowl of noodle soup. In order to move to each following stop I tap a small floating cat collar. The next stop offers a short history of the arrival of Vietnamese migrants to Britain after the victory of Ho Chi Minh's People's Army in 1975, provided by archive television footage made available in 1970s virtual televisions that suddenly populate my smartphone screen. This is followed by testimonies of later generations learning Vietnamese as a form of reconnection. Further along I witness a discussion on the importance of cross-generational conversations enabled by exploring practices of home gardening. By the end of the walk, the cat has established her Vietnamese origins, and viewers also learn that 2023 will be the year of the cat in Vietnamese lunar calendar. Here the augmented reality mixes 1970s televisions, hanging representations of the Vietnamese Zodiac chart and three-dimensional versions of people offering their testimonies or food recommendations as well as archival film footage.

Insofar as Storytrail's focus more broadly is organised around 'town squares, local libraries, streets and cinemas' and evidently on the changed twenty-first-century racial make-up of and indeed migration to Britain, elements of this project bear similarities to its in 1951 predecessor (Unboxed, 2022). Aesthetically, the visual juxtaposition of innovative AR technologies and contemporary environments with archival material and vintage furniture design calls to mind Conekin's assessment of the pavilion's linking of the present and past, even if the past represented here is more recent. The interactivity afforded by AR similarly offers viewers a multisensory engagement with locality and history which is reminiscent of the interactive screen of the pavilion, although technological advances make this engagement even more embodied. Amanda Murphy, Story-Trails' executive producer, explains that the project sought to innovate in its use of archives through the scanning of objects and people, inserting film into the environment and giving people the sense of experiencing history as and where it happened (Best in Heritage). It also gave participants the opportunity to insert themselves into a local 'people's map' through three-dimensional scanning technologies – their stories about local spaces now immortalised in small video clips on the project's website. Thus, the focus on minoritarian histories supplemented with personal vignettes relating to local sites highlights a new set of diversities, strongly impacted by migration in the London examples. Finally, the integration of figures such as Olive Morris similarly seeks to frame some of the project's historical exploration through narrations of struggle for justice, which in the context of Story-Trails being a representation of 'our history' similarly folds these struggles into a particular understanding of British freedoms. Yet it is also when read alongside the backdrop of the British government's discourses on race and the policing of migration that lineages to earlier evocation of British identity reveal themselves.

Revisiting the legislative expansion of migration law since 1951 offers an austere counterpoint to the array of differences presented in Story-Trails. While official celebrations of historical migration now abound, including the 2013 Liberal-Conservative government-backed institution of Windrush day on the 22 of June of each year, the ever-tightening restrictions imposed on migrants led to the widely deplored 'Windrush Scandal'. This was a direct result of Theresa May's 'hostile environment' policy, which widened immigration checks across many sectors of society and concerned the treatment of older Caribbean migrants who suddenly were treated as illegal immigrants despite having a 'right of abode' (Bhattacharyya et.al: 18). Their universally decried treatment is directly linked to the 1948 act and its successive reversal in the 1971 Immigration Act. The 1971 act had ended the right of colony and Commonwealth citizens to enter Britain but granted the right of abode to those already settled in Britain (El-Enany: 117). The subsequent 1981 act fully articulated the category of British citizenship as bound by Britain and the North of Ireland's contemporary borders through restricting it to children born in the country to a British parent (126). These shifts in policy led many to not take up their right to register for British citizenship, resulting in their sudden recategorisation as undocumented migrants under the 2014 Conservative government's Immigration Act. Conceived by then Home Secretary Theresa May, the act shifted the border into the everyday fabric of British life, as 'the government made proof of legal status mandatory for access to the basic means of existence: employment, housing, healthcare, education, a bank account, a driving licence' (Bhattacharyya et.al.: 18). As El-Enany argues, this series of acts serve to 'divorce Britain conceptually and physically from its former colonies', a process which also affected the parallel shifts in refugee and asylum law throughout the same period (126). Despite the fact that most asylum seekers in Britain are from its former colonies, this severing of Britain from its empire and 'the acceptance of the distinction between categories such as "refugee" and "migrant" thus allows Britain to conceal its colonial history beneath a veneer of humanitarianism' (134) Drawing attention to the colonial context in which legal status is bestowed to maintain a racially ordered Britain, she also folds in the selectivity of refugee law with its narrow criteria in determining individuals' right to remain. Recent governmental projects such as the failed plans to process asylum seekers in Rwanda point to the extreme manner through which contemporary practices are built on evocations of 'the bogus refugee'. Yet the humanitarian veneer of refugee law towards certain displaced people participates in maintaining a national image of a benevolent and rule-based state. Furthermore, for all the conceptual difficulties in distinguishing between 'migrants' and 'refugees', such distinctions create specific modes of victimisation which help decide which type of asylum seeker exactly deserves Britain's generous helping hand.

2.3 Representing Exceptional Differences in 2022

In this regard, the focus on Vietnamese immigration for the flagship AR walk for Lewisham is notable. Vietnam was never directly colonised by Britain but in the period between 1975 and the early 1990s, many Vietnamese people fled the country to reach the then British colony of Hong Kong. In parts this was due to economic hardship and authoritarianism experienced in Vietnam, but also the specific victimisation and subsequent exile of ethnic Chinese populations after China's invasion in 1978. The largest influx of Vietnamese refugees to Britain was in 1979, as Margaret Thatcher agreed to accommodate 10,000 people who had been stranded in Hong Kong's ever-expanding camps. In 2009 however, papers revealed that far from constituting a magnanimous gesture by the Prime Minister, Thatcher had to be convinced to act by her home and foreign secretaries. Thatcher had stated concerns about council house resources and favoured hosting 'Rhodesians, Poles and Hungarians, since they could more easily be assimilated into British society' (Tran, 2009). These revelations echo El-Enany's arguments that British migration policies favour white Commonwealth citizens and Europeans. The choice of foregrounding Vietnamese migration in *StoryTrails* also points to the severing of the links between migration and formerly colonised territories while bolstering an image of the state's humanitarian benevolence towards people fleeing a violent and ideologically suspect regime. Relieved of any (direct) historical links to Vietnamese colonisation, the British state is thus made to appear fair in how it grants asylum to a people detached from its own (direct) imperial endeavours. Britain appears as a hospitable land whose charitable actions have enabled thriving communities within its metropolis, enriching the local cultures through novel culinary and religious traditions. This narrative is, however, immediately contradicted by historical fact: the original choices made in 1979 by the government was to disperse Vietnamese migrants across the whole of the country rather than letting new groups of migrants settle together, such as is presented in the walk through the evocations of a locally defined community. This image of Britain also sits jarringly with the fact that Vietnamese migrants are currently the largest group of people risking their lives in small boat Channel crossings and that in 2019, thirty-nine of these migrants were found dead from hypothermia in a refrigerated lorry in Essex.

New Cat affords an insight on how certain representations of migration unwittingly entrench the full severance of Britain from the Commonwealth in terms of migration policy, while upholding it as a land of asylum for a specific selection of deserving refugees. *Winnie's Walk* arguably achieves something similar, presenting as it does contemporary understandings of Britain's internal racial ordering and how these mirror shifts in understandings of difference which do not unsettle the hardening logics of the state's migratory policies. Despite arriving in Britain before 1948, Winifred Atwell would have been folded into the expanded category of citizen after her arrival from Trinidad in 1946. Pamela Graham has described Atwell as a 'famous forgotten' figure, and her numerous achievements are noteworthy (2019). As well as being the first Black woman to achieve a number one single in the national charts, she was also the first to have her own named television show in 1957 and she performed at the Royal Variety Performance in 1952 (116). As noted by the walk, she also opened one of the first Black Hair salons in London, displaying savvy entrepreneurship while providing a vital service for the growing Black community of the 1950s. Despite not being a prominent anti-racist activist, she linked her comfortable experience of Britain as a Black woman to her wealth. She also spoke out against the treatment and segregation of Aborigine populations in Australia where she eventually settled in 1970, in parts due to increasing racist tensions in Britain. While *Winnie's Walk* never explicitly claims she is a part of this generation of migrants, the location of the walk is noteworthy, departing from Windrush square to wander around Brixton, an area which is itself most iconic of the post-war settlement of Caribbean communities in Britain. As the mid-century furniture appears amidst the rapidly gentrifying streets and remainders of the area's last seventy years of Black history and understood in conjunction with the popular framing of the 'Windrush generation', here too the present becomes linked in a certain sense of the past. This past is not a millennium away, but still a vison that in its earnest desire to uncover a forgotten yet remarkable life story inevitably frames Brixton's historical Black population as a part of an exceptionally deserving part of Britain's diverse fabric. The question of exceptionality becomes even more resonant when considered with regard to socially sanctioned anti-racist practices.

Graham traces how the expansion of digital tools has enabled the deserved remembering of Atwell as an important figure and *StoryTrails*' audiowalk participates in this recovery. However, both Atwell's life story and the specific location of the audiowalk display a certain selectivity regarding which categories of migrants might deserve to be highlighted as intrinsic to Britain's (multi) cultural fabric, and to what ends. Despite Atwell's earlier arrival she is read as being a part of the recently victimised 'Windrush generation', a shorthand denomination for all Black migrants settled in the country prior to the 1971 immigration act (Graham: 117). Prior to, but especially during the unfolding of the scandalous revelation of the consequences of May's 'hostile environment' policy, the country saw a vocal and surprising political outcry over their treatment. Surprising because, as noted by the authors of Empire's Endgame many 'were black and many of them worked in lower-income jobs or were welfare claimants. This is the same economic demographic – 'benefit scroungers' and 'job stealers' – who are the target of popular outrage in debates about immigration (19). The authors note that in opposition to these usual depictions, 'victims of the Windrush scandal were portrayed as elderly, respectable and law-abiding, and the well-rehearsed yarn about them having been invited over to help with the post-war effort prevailed' (19). These reactions obscure both the institutional and violent street racism faced by these individuals upon arrival and in the years to follow, an obstruction also at play in the retroactive renaming of these migrants as the 'Windrush Generation'. The public outcry also serves as a misremembering of the initial purpose of the expansion of British citizenship, which had more to do with maintaining the empire than inviting new Black citizens to rebuild its core. This misremembering thus operates as a mechanism to integrate former outsiders to the nation into prior understandings of British diversity without unsettling its bounded and bordered insularity. Now understood as settled, orderly and respectable, the Windrush generation 'were folded into the national 'we', reclaimed as *our* war veterans, *our* bus conductors and *our* caring nurses' (19).

While the forgotten fame of Atwell is indicative of an evident racist selectivity in historical practices of memorialisation, her story is presented as a tale of resilience linked to individual talent. Beyond her artistic and commercial achievements, she overcame Australia's 'white only' policy and was allowed to settle in the country (Graham: 117). This adds to the heroic nature of her life's journey, while her hair salon also presents her as an adaptable migrant able to deftly integrate into her host country's commercial fabric. Her story comes to stand in for a certain sanitised version of Brixton, which in turn implicitly makes her stand in for the Windrush generation. Indeed the overall intent of this walk is grounded in a politics of representation, which situates the overcoming of racism – and other forms of identity-based oppression – in the increased visibility of people of colour in sites of political power and in media. This strategy thus often relies 'on a reading of anti-racist histories which both begins with post-war migration and remains focused on the confines of European nation states' which in turn imagines 'politics as a bounded community where to be included is to overcome racism' (Bhattacharyya et.al.: 49–50). This strategy operates in parallel with the rupture of migration policies from histories of imperial domination. According to Koram, this representative anti-racism always runs risk of situating legacies of Empire within 'the symbolic and cultural register'. He does not dismiss the importance of cultural representation – nor do I – but does draw attention to how focusing on representation alone ignores imperial legacies plaguing many communities in Britain today (12). Thus, harnessing narratives of either exemplary or victimised migrants in public cultural narratives such as *StoryTrails* appears like less of a contradiction than the extreme xeno-racist context of contemporary Britain might initially suggest. As Toscano argues: 'Neoliberalism operates through a racial state ... shaped by a racist and civilisational imaginary that delimits who is capable of market freedoms' (2024: 73–74). This in turn enacts 'a *differential* reinforcement of the state, which in turn compounds and refunctions those "fatal couplings of power and difference" that, according to Stuart Hall, define the making, unmaking and remaking of *race*' (71). While clearly the Windrush generation and their children are not 'protected' – following from the Gilmore's diagnosis of the state's material practices, the retroactive mythologisation of certain racialised categories of people always runs risk of distracting from the sacrifice of others. Even projects such as *StoryTrails* that are evidently grounded in real desire to celebrate a more expansive notion of Britishness can never fully elide the trap of the racialised ordering El-Enany acutely identifies as being foundational to post-imperial bordered Britain.

Koram's assessment of the persistent and multipronged afterlife of Empire as it manifests on British soil brings me briefly back to Catford as an exemplary site to diagnose the effects of such afterlives. In December 2020, coroner Philip Barlow ruled that the air pollution form the South Circular Road in Catford was the primary cause of nine-year-old Black girl Ella Kissi-Debrah's death from acute asthma in 2013 (Laville, 2020). Meanwhile a 2023 report from the Institute for Fiscal Studies noted that despite a significant drop over the past twenty years, the 'ethnic pollution gap' still stood at 6 per cent, with Black communities most affected by exposure to fine particulate matter resulting from domestic fuel burning, road transport and industrial processes (Gadenne et al., 2024). Like the example of Grenfell which opened this section, the death of Kissi-Debrah in an area of Lewisham where most inhabitants are not ethnically white British and 27.5 per cent are of Black heritage is a stark reminder of Ruth Wilson Gilmore's definition of racism as 'the state-sanctioned or extralegal production and exploitation of group-differentiated vulnerability to premature death' (Wilson-Gilmore, 2007: 247). For all of Olusoga's well-meaning desire to honour the country's multicultural fabric of 2022 Britain, individualised histories distract from the material urban backdrop in which they manifest, alongside current technologies of racial ordering. As I have argued through my use of El-Enany, Koram and *Empire's Endgame*', these technologies are intimately tied to practices of bordering as they intersect with day-to-day social interactions and the organisation of urban environments of Britain's cities where tower blocks most likely stand by dual carriageways and, through dangerous cladding, are turned into death traps for the cosmetic satisfaction of wealthier neighbours. Reckoning with empire cannot solely rely on processes of recovery, which in their very naming signal that imperialism ceased with the historical decolonisation of the 1920s–1960s. Rather, empire still structures the lethal, if often slow, material realities of many racialised people's lives in Britain and beyond. As Koram argues: 'Empire carries an economic legacy, not just a cultural or racial one' (17). I will analyse some of this economic legacy in my following section – a consideration of the artistic representation of extractive practices within the festivals of 1951 and 2022. Indeed, the relationship between current practices and companies, most notably BP, are inevitably enmeshed in longer histories and current manifestations of imperialist economic dispossession.

However I would like to briefly conclude my exploration with another contemporary narrativisation of Black British history, this time in Steve Mc Queen's 2020 TV film *Mangrove* as a counterexample, via considerations of the state offered in the introduction. As further noted by the PPE collective, as a supplementary mediator of class conflict, the state interpellates individuals through cultural representations, unifying them into the singular entity of 'the people' (Blackwell-Pal et al., 2021: 46). This use of representation is evident in the Lion and Unicorn and *Storytrails* in which particularised communities' historical struggles against the state, come to be folded into the very narrative of the state's present embrace of differences. In his exploration of the difficulties posed by the diverse definitions of 'popular culture' Stuart Hall situates it as embodied in popular traditions and practices which remain in tension to the dominant culture of the power block (Hall, 1981). This approach offers a generative frame to consider how art might otherwise manifest these tensions when working with histories of resistance without risking a retroactive incorporation into celebratory narratives of progressive change. McQueen's *Mangrove* offers an example of one such strategy. The film focuses on the case of the Mangrove 9, Black radical activists from London charged and then cleared of inciting a riot in 1970. Throughout the film, Grenfell Tower lingers in the background, covered in tarp, most prominently in a protest scene. The tower was not yet built in 1970, and leaving its present shadow in the background seems like a purposeful act by McQueen who could easily have scrubbed it in post-production. While convivial and successful narratives of multiculturalism might offer a mirage of a widely tolerant Britain, it is crucially images like this one that more urgently articulate its deathly organised racial and capitalist violence – and forms of resistance to it.

3 Extractive Labours

Upon entering Kelvin Hall on Glasgow's Argyle Street in 1951, visitors of the FOB's Industrial Power Exhibition would encounter Scotland's largest sculpture, a gigantic replica of coal cliff by Thomas Whalen. To the left, above the entrance leading to the coal section of the exhibition looms 'the good of Nature', with his sunlike head and arm outstretched. On the left, man 'awakened and digging in the coal seams while at the centre water and air figure as the essential elements without which 'trees and ferns could not have undergone the changes which caused them to break down into the beginnings of coal' (IPE catalogue, 1951: 8) (see Figure 3). This grandiose entrance to the exhibition is an unabashed celebration of human mastery over nature, the god 'urging Man (*sic*) to win coal 'and make it its servant' (IPE catalogue, 1951: 8). Seventy-one years later, I find myself queuing on a late October day by Weston-super-Mare's windy shore, looking up to a decommissioned oil platform repurposed as an energetically self-sustaining installation named *Seemonster*, Unboxed's last project to open to the public in late September 2022. Enthusiastic locals surround me, as I overhear stories of prior visits. While *Seemonster*'s thematic concerns pertain to notions of Britishness in relationship to the weather, the repurposing of the extractive platform as a comment on green transition and reuse is evidently at the forefront – a very different approach to resource extraction than the bold glorification of coal presented at the IPE.

The contrasting relationship to fossil fuels and technological progress displayed in both events is hardly surprising given their temporal distance and the centrality of the nationalisation of the mining industry by Attlee's government compared with current understandings of coal's damaging ecological effects. Thus comparing both works is a generative exercise in tracing Britain's relationship to extractivist and industrial practices and how these might map onto older imperial models. What also links them both are their differing representations of labour. In Glasgow, the toil of men (and it was only men) was central to

Figure 3 Industrial Power Exhibition – Kelvin Hall – Hall of Power designed by Basil Spence (1951). Curtesy of the National Archives, Kew.

the exhibition and miners were explicitly employed to demonstrate aspects of their work as part of the exhibition. In Weston, conversely, any mention of offshore labourers and their function as a part of oil drilling or green transitions out of it was fully absent from *Seemonster*'s general evocation of self-sustenance. This raises questions about what the obscuring of labour signifies for current understandings of the climate crisis and technologies to fix it. In view of this, illuminating how extraction was understood just over seventy years ago offers a generative point of departure.

3.1 Coal Is Power

While the idea of the Festival of Britain itself and the Lion and Unicorn Pavilion might imply that its principal focus was on exploring expressions of British identity through art and design, one of its central remits was to showcase a national history which stressed scientific and technological progress. The design and architectural innovations are not be overlooked, especially when the only permanent structure that remains of it is the Royal Festival Hall, yet art was often deployed in a supporting role to make narrations of scientific progress accessible. Nowhere was this celebration of Britain's extractive and industrial achievements more evident than at the Glasgow Industrial Power Exhibition

(IPE). One of the least successful exhibits of the festival in terms of visitors – a key blame being laid on the masculine appeal of its topic – its purpose was to narrate the history and centrality of water and coal to Britain's industrial prowess, before ending its journey with the promise of atomic energy in 'the Hall of the Future'. The original plan to hold the event as a 'live exhibition' focused on shipbuilding was dropped due to the impractical necessity to shuttle visitors across sites – however some performed work demonstrations are included in the coal section in its final iteration. Here, Scottish miners with different skills are seen operating machinery and 'doing their stint in conditions approximating as closely as the ingenuity of architects and artists can make them to those which exist in a typical British mine' (11). In an additional move to replicate elements of their working conditions, visitors are invited to descend from the Hall of Power 'to a pit working level in standard cages' who 'like the men who work them, are the real thing and will be employed in the Scottish coalfields when the exhibition ends' (10–11). A BBC segment confirms this inclusion of workers, noting: 'Even the operator of the pit cage is authentic – Albert Hamble was temporarily laid off from the colliery where he works after it flooded' (BBC On This Day, no date).

The catalogue describes the exhibition as having been planned to tell the story of Britain's tremendous contribution to heavy engineering. In focusing not only on machines but the men who made them and people who use them, it 'sets out to show not only British inventiveness, but the effect it has had on the world' (1951: 7). As opposed to the pavilion, this exhibition is structured around two distinct routes visitors can take. Starting in the great Hall of Power, and after passing a doorway featuring a crackling artificial sun, visitors are invited to pick as their first topic either water ('hydroelectricity') or coal. Visitors are told that it doesn't matter which sequence is followed first as water and coal's rhythm of progress differs, but that the overall story will unfold logically (8). However, placing water and coal at the very start of the journey presents them as the central drivers of British economic success and their harnessing informs subsequent displays focusing on steel, railways and shipbuilding, power for industry and electricity. The latter part of the exhibition moves onto the prowess of British civil engineering, exploring successful projects carried out across West Africa and Egypt – another muted reference to Britain's empire. It finally concludes in the Hall of the Future, a celebration of the 'peaceful deployment of atomic energy' and Britain's contributions to it. While not as large in scale as the South Bank exhibition, describing each of the IPE's elements in much detail is beyond the scope of this Element, and my argument will focus primarily on its deployment of miners and its approach to atomic energy in the final Hall of the Future, both of which I will describe in more detail next.

These components of the IPE offer many moments that invite unpicking: performances of labour, the by now somewhat uncomfortable glorification of coal as primary fuel of British prosperity and the hopeful promise of nuclear energy. I will consider of each these elements in turn but also the way labour can connect them, before turning to 2022's repurposed oil rig *Seemonster*. Yet first I want to turn to centrality of the industrial revolution and its consequences in the form of drastic climate change. The role of the industrial revolution, as the exhibition makes clear, is fundamental not only to Britain's relative wealth but also to its colonising efforts. However, the determining role of Britain can remain underplayed or somewhat dissimulated under the vaguer sounding term Anthropocene, implicating humanity universally in environmental degradation. Stemming from the field of Geography and popularised over the course of the last twenty years, Anthropocene has broadly come to designate the geological epoch in which general human activity has become the dominant catalyst in geological and ecological change. Yet Andreas Malm observes that in 1850, 'Britain emitted nearly twice as much carbon dioxide as the US, France, Germany and Belgium combined. If global warming has a historical homeland, there can indeed be no doubt about its identity' (2016: 309). He notes that a cotton manufacturer from Lancashire who decided to forgo his waterwheel in favour of a steam engine in the early nineteenth century would have not known the long-reaching consequences of this choice. The organisers of the Glasgow exhibition would similarly not yet be fully informed of the impact of industry at this gigantic a scale, although some issues related to local pollution are pointed to in the catalogue (IPE catalogue: 1–2).

What is, however, curious is the presentation of industrial progress as a collective British endeavour. As Malm further argues steam engines were not adopted by some natural-born deputies of the human species but rather by the owners of the means of production. He observes that these were an all-male, and all-white class of people comprising an 'infinitesimal fraction of the population of *Homo sapiens* in the early nineteenth century' (325). Thus, Malm argues that Anthropogenic climate change 'has its roots *outside* the realm of temperature and precipitation, turtles and polar bears, inside a sphere of human praxis that could be summed up in one word as *labour*' (12). Furthermore, the mode of organisation of this labour in the context of nineteenth-century Britain is shaped by its gradual alignment with the formalisation of a capitalist socio-economic system. The move from using water to using coal for steam meant that for the owners of industry, the labour process could be structurally altered to increase productivity through a fundamental transformation of the production process itself. This process is called real subsumption and describes the instance by which beyond simply profiting from an existing labour process, capital fundamentally transforms it. The development of time-saving steam engines enabled not only higher productivity but also the ability to move factories to places across the country with higher supplies of cheap labour such as cities. While water is immune to real subsumption because unproduced by human labour, coal can only be picked by humans. From shifting from water to steam 'capital necessarily became *more dependent on human labour* in one very special sphere: the production of energy itself' (377). Although Britain's emissions are now dwarfed by contemporary global powers such as China and the United States, Adam Hanieh notes that the adoption of coal as the world's primary fuel was a fundamental driver of 'multiple logics of the new capitalism that Britain embodied and led at the time' – meaning that between 1870 and 1900, capitalism became irrevocably fossilised (2024: 19). The FOB's choice of privileging the display of extractive work in the IPE could have stemmed from the exhibition's original conception as one of heavy industry, the South Bank being the preferred site for the replication of commodity manufacturing assembly lines. Yet it is not only the difference with the South Bank that is noteworthy here but also how the display of technical mining work relates to earlier examples of worker's displays at universal exhibits and activist traditions of demonstrating sweated labour.

3.2 Looking at Workers

Displaying human activity in the context of European modernity was not specific to the FOB. As well as the objectifying racist traditions of human zoos that proliferated across Western world fairs up until the middle of the twentieth century, the 1851 London and 1867 Paris Great Exhibitions also presented displays of manual waged labour. Despite serving as showcases for national technological progress, many world fairs and exhibitions preferred to showcase skills that involved work practices not yet fully mechanised. This may have been linked to the advertisement of luxury artisanal products, yet this choice was also underpinned by certain moral panics which surrounded factory work at the time. Adrian Rifkin offers some interesting reflections regarding French representations of such displays at the 1867 Paris exhibition. He notes the inclusion of demonstrations of the 'petits métiers' – specialist handmade crafts, such as lacemaking, hat-making or jewellery – observing that viewers could enjoy two illusions at least:

> One was the appearance of the relative independence and self-motivation of the workers. The appearance that is, because, in the case of the lacemakers, they belonged to home-based industries controlled by a single large capitalist. ... Another illusion was the absence of industrial disease. (Rifkin, 1985: 24)

This display had been organised by the event's director, Le Play, an opponent of social progress who favoured the development of modern industry, thus finding lasting values in the moral sphere which he located in the rural family unit (24). Rifkin reads these specific displays as an image of labour made both to defend itself and to hold it in its social place. Images of skilled workers glorified forms of manual labour, and implied that their dignity stemmed from an understanding of their place in the labour process (27; 20).

Conversely, practices of representing sweated labour also developed to expose and reform the factory conditions of hyper-exploited workers employed in the low-cost sector of clothing production. Sheila Blackburn traces the evolution of this phenomenon, originally exposed in journalistic reports and novels. She considers their deployments first as written narratives and subsequently live displays attempting to reproduce the appalling environments and lives of sweated workers as a campaigning tool for a range of socialist groups and initiatives. She notes the shift in understandings of identity of sweated labourers from the mid nineteenth century through to 1906 from 'the lone, pathetic, but deserving shirtmaker', its existence being blamed on the slavish amoral Irish and 'anti-social' Jewish immigrants. This archetypical image of the sweated labourer was the unskilled and defenceless female homeworker. This understanding persisted until 1906 when activists organised an exhibition at Queen's Hall in London displaying workers of all genders, highlighting that sweated labour was in fact the prevailing condition in the lower echelons of the British workforce (Blackburn: 40). This realisation coincided with the moment activists decided to use the live display of sweated work as a campaigning tool.

Both examples, grounded in contrasting but equally invested arguments for maintaining dignified conditions, also show how the exhibition of 'authentic' workers in a staged work environment was understood to be a compelling method of persuasion. Demonstrations of sweated labour in particular are in line with the 1951 narration of a labour inflected vision of British history. The mining section of the Glasgow exhibition includes panels describing the evolution of safety measures and points to historically appalling work condition in mines, before visitors are led to 'the principal display, where miners demonstrate the latest methods of coal-cutting by machinery' (IPE catalogue: 11). The inclusion of a 'live' mining element thus signals how the newly nationalised coal industry – producing 90 per cent of Britain's energy supplies in 1951 – made Britain a world leader in coal mining and promised radically less lethal working conditions. However, as opposed to sweated labour displays, integrating aspects of the live labour process also seems to evoke 'honest work', albeit one in which technology and the state have tamed the corrupting influence of machines to offer a harmonious and risk-free vision of social democratic progress. The inclusion of 'the real thing' doesn't seem straightforwardly grounded in a moralistic championing of artisanal work or conversely a denunciation of exploitative labour conditions. Rather, the 'real thing' provided by the miners was a means to celebrate the toil of those who heroically kept Britain's energy supplies running.

This celebration of the miner is evident in the National Coal Board's (NCB) *Mining Review*'s 1951 September issue featuring a report on the IPE documenting the live display showcasing contemporary technological advances. The short report – titled *The Key to Power* – starts by depicting large crowds moving through the Hall of Power and proudly announces that half the exhibition focuses on coal. The film introduces the viewer to the IPE's re-creation of a 'primeval' forest, the origins of the fuel, before jumping to the early development of coal extraction in superficial shafts. The film then moves on to the industrial revolution, announcing that the 'coming of steam meant more coal, deeper shafts and the first winding engine' (Pickering & Tharpe, 1951). Viewers are then shown images of the exhibitions' models depicting a miserable looking child and adult miners, the latter hand pulling carriages, the voiceover decrying that a 100 years ago 'this was still common', that 'safety regulations were unheard of' and 'disasters were everyday news' (Mining Review, 1951). As visitors move past a carved wall seeming to depict humans trapped in constricted underground pockets, the story finally 'moves us out of this nightmare and right into the present' as the camera turns towards the cage that journeys people down into the replica of a modern mine (Mining Review, 1951). As the film focuses on people's descent, the music switches from a tense and ominous orchestral arrangement to a smoother melody and finally, mechanised mining is on show. The Meco-Moore cutter loader is hailed as one of Scotland's contributions to greater and safer outputs. Excited groups of children gather around a mining railway powered by diesel, followed by a short cut to 'a samson loader too that draws the crowds as it clutters into action', another Scottish made machine (Mining Review, 1951). As the segment concludes, the camera lingers on the proud statue of a miner and hails the Kelvinhall display as 'the most complete exhibition on mining that we've seen. It shows us the miner, something of his struggle and his achievements and reminds us that coal and the men who mine it are keystones of Britain's industrial power' (Mining Review, 1951). In the final moments, a man dressed in full mining gear passes a sign stating 'Coal is Power' (Mining Review, 1951).

The nationalisation of the coal industry in 1947 was a flagship policy of Attlee's government, underpinned by the necessity of increasing energy production to support post-war reconstruction. According to Huw Beynon and Ray Hudson, the prevailing view was that the promise of nationalisation would be enough to tackle absenteeism and push productivity (2021: 57). The process was not that smooth; tensions around wages and working conditions raised by unions exposed the fact that nationalising the industry itself would not be incentive enough to convince miners to redouble efforts and cease striking. An agreement was reached on 1 January 1947, mining was taken into public ownership and the NCB formed. The National Union of Miners was directly involved in constructing the formal apparatus of the NCB, bringing 'coal owner, mine manager and union official together as administrators of the industry' (52). Although 1951 is now understood as the dawn of the age of oil, between 1947 and 1957 coal production increased from 193 to 227 million tonnes yearly, in parts due to changes in social and technical production (56). This production drive was accompanied by a new heroic view of the miner orchestrated by the state corporation, celebrated in effigies at union festivals, notably the Durham Miners' Gala – attended amongst others by the US ambassador (60). Key to this state sanctioned celebration of the new social-democratic nation's cornerstone industry were the NCB's monthly *Mining Review* reels, documenting multiple aspects of mining life in cinemas and communities across the country. This lionisation of miners and promotion of Britain's technological advances are evident in the *Mining Review*'s 'The Key to Power', implicitly championing the social democratic compact in its condemnation of nineteenth-century exploitation and casualties and display of cutting-edge machinery alongside the friendly miners demonstrating their use.

Yet for all the alleged promises that nationalisation would improve working conditions expressed through the refiguration of the miner as a working-class hero essential to the nation's rejuvenation, the industry's safety did not improve significantly from the immediate pre-war years. Beynon and Hudson argue that despite some hopes that union involvement and technological progress might improve workplace safety, coal shortages created pressures for increased production and expenditure restrictions did nothing to alleviate working conditions or the rate of accidents (63). Meanwhile by 1950 deaths by pneumoconiosis outnumbered accidents by a ratio of four to one. Yet the NCB decided to allow men diagnosed with the condition return to work in 1951 due to labour shortages, indicating that the production of coal took priority over concerns for welfare (64). Additionally, despite the integration of union leaders into the composition of the coal board itself industrial unrest continued, mostly driven by contests to the piece-work earning system; 1948 saw 1,528 work stoppages, many of them unsanctioned by the NUM. Thus in considering the performances of mining practices at the IPE, one can find echoes of Rifkin's argument. Nowhere does the question of industrial disease appear in the catalogue or the reel and the continued safety challenges of mining work are obscured through showcasing unevenly implemented time and life-saving technologies. For all the expressions of working-class pride operating as a symbolic challenge to Britain's social Victorian social stratification and the illusion of dignified working conditions, here again we see an image of labour being held in its social place; indeed as the concurrent strikes indicate, no amount of exalted celebrations of dignified miners as saviours of the nation's prosperity could make-up for bad working conditions. In contrast, discussions of nuclear power were presented in a more cautious manner relatively to these sanitised images of the mining industry.

3.3 Atoms and Wind Turbines

Whichever route visitors chose to take in journey across Kelvinhall, their paths rejoin in the final Hall of the Future, a celebration of the promise of nuclear energy for a possible coming 'age of plenty and comfort' (IPE catalogue, 45). In a similar manner to the Lion and Unicorn Pavilion, past, present and future are melded to provide a promethean vision of British progress, underlined here by a spectacular representation of atomic power:

> On entering the Hall of the Future, the visitor walks in the present, looks down on the past, and looks up to the future. In a series of pits below floor level the great pioneers of the past are seen at work. Above is a shining cone rising from the floor, its tip pulsating and throwing off great crackling flashes of lightning to a night sky which curves above it in a twinkling hemisphere-the limitless future. (42)

This selection of engineers and scientists encapsulates the thematic concerns of the exhibition, tracing British innovations in engineering from early inventions all the way to that of Ernest Rutherford's, who in 1912 discovered the structure of the atom – a key motif in the whole festival which I will return to in the final section. However, for all the hall's grandiosity, Conekin remarks 'that the problematic nature of the new source of power was not entirely glossed over' (1999: 243). Indeed in the concluding remarks on this section, the catalogue notes that this discovery: 'will determine whether we are entering an age of undreamed-of plenty and comfort, or whether we are working out our complete extinction' (45). She notes the double-edged discussion of atomic energy was atypical with regard to contemporaneous assessments which simply presented nuclear progress 'as the solution to every kind of modern-day problem' (243). The development of the atomic bomb will in fact turn out to have an unexpected relationship to the FOB which I will return to in the final section. Yet it is also another omission that in retrospect feels striking: the near absence of discussions of oil. Hanieh indicates that by the mid twentieth century, global consumption of oil had surpassed that of coal including in Western Europe' (19). By 1962 Britain had become the largest petrochemicals producer in Europe (Marriott and Macalister: 57). As civil and martial uses of nuclear power have also continued to increase, the hopefulness of the atomic age has been replaced by an ambivalence premised on the threat posed by atomic weapons and problems posed by the waste it produces. Oil, however, has come to dominate not only industry and electricity production but the materials of our everyday existence, from road and air transport all the way to microplastics. As the past seventy years have seen the full establishment of a global petroculture, oil has played a crucial part of British political and economic development, a role that I will turn to after considering a monument to its supposed disappearance, Unboxed's *Seemonster*.

So let's jump forward to the cold October day I travelled to the shores of the Bristol Channel, to visit a somewhat different image of extraction. *Seemonster* was the last of Unboxed's offerings to be launched. It consisted of a decommissioned North Sea oil platform shipped from the Netherlands to Weston Super Mare, described by its creators as 'a joyous celebration of the great British weather and British eccentricity' (Seemonster, 2022). Ironically delayed by difficult weather conditions, it missed its original opening date in late August, although the planned inaugural drone shows did go ahead as planned. It fully opened one month later. *Seemonster* was conceived by Newsubstance, a creative studio based in Leeds whose drone division SkyMagic also delivered the opening spectacle. They describe themselves as 'diverse, disruptive and driven' and both companies stress their expertise in joining technology and creativity. In developing the project, they worked with a series of collaborators, most notably Dr Amélie Kirchgaessner and Dr Ella Gilbert, researchers at the British Antarctic Survey who were approached due to their 'positive outlook', no mean feat in the field of climate science. Weston super Mare itself is a small town in the Bristol Channel in the South West of England. It saw an expansion in the nineteenth century as a popular seaside resort, before starting to decline towards the end of the twentieth. As opposed to Glasgow, its economic and cultural importance could be conceived as peripheral at best, and over the past twenty years seaside towns on the English coast such as Weston have become symbols of dereliction, destitution and in some cases resolutely xenophobic politics. Often framed as places in need of economic and cultural regeneration, such towns offer a very different evocation of working-class culture than the celebratory 1951 Scottish display. While, of course, the development of nineteenth-century seaside leisure is fundamentally intertwined with economic shifts towards colonial extraction and industrial capitalism, the spaces of Weston super Mare also do not bear the most evident traces of this aspect of British history that populate both Glasgow and London landscapes.

Seemonster was explicitly oriented towards ecological sustainability, invested in demonstrating how a former oil rig, a paradigmatic symbol of advanced fossil fuel extraction, could be repurposed into an energetically self-sufficient installation gesturing towards a green, net zero future. The installation itself consists of a garden maintained by reusable sources produced by eco sculptures Solar Tree and the WindNest used to power the irrigation system at various levels of the platform, making the structure self-sustainable in terms of energy consumption. The installation is impressive: as noted by BBC Somerset, the entire structure is 35 m tall – 15 m taller than the Angel of the North. Upon arrival in Weston, *Seemonster* is rapidly visible above the roofs of the city, the wind-responsive kinetic scales that adorn its exterior shimmering in the afternoon light. After a relatively lengthy queue, I am finally invited to take my journey up a series of levels, a waterfall gushing down the structure opposite the stairs. The cellar deck is renamed 'Cloud Portal', describing the large circular contraption on the ceiling that produces a damp mist floating above and around visitors. The top deck meanwhile contains a garden lab above both fostering and enabled by renewable energy technology, and hosting beds of coastal shrubs and trees. Amongst the plants stand one yellow and one white kinetic sculptures designed by Ivan Black, stems topped with assembled geometric panels moving in relationship to the wind and each other. The renewable energy sources Solar Tree and WindNest also have sculptural qualities, the former looking like an upturned gramophone horn and the latter dissimulating two small wind turbines in white and orange pods. At the very top of the rig, on what would have been the helideck, visitors can access a slide to swiftly return to the Cloud Portal if they wished, a popular option on the day I visit. The helipad itself is reshaped into a small outdoor auditorium where I am invited to sit and listen to the shipping forecast and observe both the town below and ever shifting sky above (see Figure 4).

This top deck's function is described by artistic director Ollie Howitt as follows:

> A place to dwell and reflect on the great British weather whilst being surrounded by it; the roaring wind, the full force of the rain and sunshine. In Britain, our lives revolve around this topic; ... Soothing sounds of the Shipping Forecast provide a nostalgic and calming setting for contemplation, bringing the British psyche to the forefront. (Seemonster)

Figure 4 Repurposed oil platform *Seemonster*, Unboxed Festival (2022). Photo by Caoimhe Mader McGuinness.

Created in 1911 and first delivered by Morse before fully moving to the radio in the 1950s, the Shipping Forecast issues weather warnings for a total of 31 'sea' regions surrounding Britain and Ireland, from Iceland through to Spain and Portugal. Tracing the history, controversies and literary works linked to the Shipping Forecast, Victoria Carolan argues that it has a strange status for a weather bulletin, becoming engrained 'as a part of British culture and as a signifier of Englishness' (2011: 104). She points to David Chandler's evocations of the podcast's 'reports of a volatile exterior against which the ideas of home and nation as places of safety, order and divine protection are reinforced' and 'rekindles a picture of Britain glowing with a sense of wholeness and unity' (104). This perceived centrality of the shipping forecast to the British psyche has led to some extensive debates, notably the change of one region's name from Finisterre to Fitzroy in 2002 – blamed on the EU –leading to lively press commentary questioning if users of the forecast had been consulted. However, as Carolan notes, 'genuine' users of the broadcast would have no use for the broadcast by 2002 with the arrival of new mobile and GPS technologies and that the Meteorological Office does not list it as a recommended resource to use. The vision of national unity here is inward looking, insular and oddly whimsical as the cultural object which appears to represent the mythical British psyche most also appears to be of no immediate discernible use beyond the mere fact of its existence. While to some this would evoke Brexit, I also want to consider how *Seemonster* might be understood when juxtaposed with aspects of the British economy in its relationship to oil extraction and empire.

In his discussion of the centrality of rentier capitalism in the UK economy, Brett Christophers draws on David Edgerton noting Britain's move from a national capitalist economy tied to an interventionist and technocratic state between the 1950s and 1970s to a place where 'world capitalism does business – no longer one where British capitalism does the world's business' (2020: 6). This shift is typically narrated as the development of financialised services and the (re)entrenchment of a rentier economy – extracting not only value from land but from infrastructure ownership all the way to natural resources. One of these natural resources happens to be North Sea oil, for which the UK to this day maintains some of the lowest taxation rates in the world after having fully privatised its shares in British Petroleum (BP) under Thatcher in 1987. Christophers notes that in a 2014 review of the oil and gas fiscal regime, the government stressed the importance of tax allowances in enabling the development of 'commercially marginal resources', steadfastly committed to enabling the greatest possible volume of fossil fuels to be extracted from the Continental shelf. Drawing on Adam Tooze, he notes that if the planned development of the North Sea goes forward it will negate many times over reductions achieved by cutting out coal (Christophers: 135). All these elements sit awkwardly with *Seemonster*'s stated aims 'to start conversations around reuse'. There is something unnerving in considering an installation so outwardly appealing to the mythologisation of a self-sustaining nation when Britain is so fundamentally held up by globalised corporate economic relationships it historically enabled.

Borrowing Aimé Césaire's concept of 'the Boomerang' – denoting the relationship between the management of colonised population and the development of European fascisms – Koram considers how long-established arrangements between corporations and the British state resulted in the corporatisation of societies across time, from postcolonial nations to Britain. Fundamental to this was Britain's lead in what Koram names 'outsourcing Empire', using private corporations which from the sixteenth century onwards did 'much of the dirty work of actually administrating Britain's vast empire' (2022: 41). This strategy would result in tensions as decolonisation gathered pace and came to a head when Iranian president Mohammed Mosaddegh nationalised Iranian oil in 1951, ending the Anglo-Iranian Oil Company's (AIOC) lucrative hold on the country's resources. While Britain owned 51 per cent of the AIOC at the time, essentially making it a nationalised company, the state partnered up with the United States to orchestrate a coup against Mosaddegh. A pro-Western regime was implemented, allowing renewed access to oil fields not only for the AIOC but also for American oil companies. As Koram argues, this early example of corporate profit undermining a decolonised nation's claim to sovereignty shows how 'corporatisation of life after empire had helped create a world in which the movement of wealth was independent of the potentially turbulent will of the demos and thus devaluing sovereignty across the board' (62). As Christophers' assessment of the current low taxation rates and concurrent enabling of continued North Sea extraction shows, the interests of the now fully privatised company remain a key concern for the British state. The AIOC rebranded as British Petroleum (BP) shortly after the 1953 coup. Despite increasingly uneven commitments by governments across the world to keep the increase of the global average temperature below 2 degree Celsius, BP has recently dropped its target to reduce oil output over the next five years and scaled back its investment in renewables (Simpson, 2024). Moreover, while an increase in windfall tax on oil companies has recently been implemented by the ruling Labour government, there is current uncertainty surrounding its potential push to approve two new drilling sites despite an election pledge to enact a full energy transition. Without wanting to doubt the sincere intentions of its makers, whatever conversations may have happened about reuse during *Seemonster*'s Weston tenure start to appear flimsy in light of evident commitments by successive governments to bow to gas and oil lobbying and encourage cheap and continued extraction of fossil fuels under their jurisdiction. *Seemonster* thus could be read as a feat of sustainable design which, perhaps like the government that funded it imagines Britain as a detached entity encircled by a volatile exterior it itself both creates and seeks out.

3.4 Looking at Magic

In a manner parallel to the softly uttered names of the shipping forecast's seafaring zones, the sea surrounding the island of Britain is divided into six offshore geographical and geological regions currently being mined for oil and gas. The first hydrocarbons started to be extracted in 1965 and by 1978 the Forties Field in the Central North Sea region was fully operational, just off the coast of Aberdeen. Yet these oil fields have remained difficult to access, and figure nearly apart from British territory proper. Marriott and Macalister note the UK North Sea was treated like a new colony by Westminster, in which far beyond the view of any citizen, a different set of rules applied (220). This assessment is not simply an evocative metaphor for yet another frontier to be conquered by intrepid Britannia: a key aspect regarding labour on these maritime platforms is that minimum wage laws did not apply 12 miles off the shore until October 2020. Interviewing the regional organiser for the Rail Maritime and Transport Workers Union (RMT) for Aberdeen shipping Jake Molloy in 2019, Marriott and Macalister describe his anger at aspects of the rig decommissioning process, as he discusses the working conditions of the Filipino crews flown in to dismantle the platforms. Working in in all weathers and temperatures, these workers are paid $45 for 12- to 15-hour shifts, less than half the UK minimum wage (278). As well as these examples of hyper-exploited migrant labour, there is a general deterioration of working conditions. Some of this can be explained by the general decline of British oil reserves since the early 2000s and to a lesser extent the push towards net zero and a green transition out of a fossil economy – although the RMT has pointed to the lack of support offered by governments to help North Sea workers retrain in renewable energy (RMT, 2025). In an echo of miner's upheavals against 1951's piecework the fact also remains that workers are increasingly hired ad hoc for two- to three-month trips, creating a 'gig economy' for highly trained individuals working in an industry where the consequences of personal error can be catastrophic (Marriot and Macalister: 277).

We are clearly at a distance from 1951's heyday for the newly nationalised King Coal which saw its energy workers manipulating extractive machinery for a paying public. Yet questions of human intervention and human labour are just as crucial to the oil industry in 2025 than they were to coal in 1951. However, any mention or representation of this labour was entirely absent from *Seemonster*, be it in any promotional material or on the platform itself. I did, of course, encounter some workers. I conversed with a security guard. As I was ready to slide down from my contemplative communion with the Shipping Forecast, a friendly usher ensured I would not land on the previous person's head. These events after all cannot go without their own fleets of casualised service workers ensuring that this unique cultural experience goes smoothly. The rig itself, however, felt scrubbed of any function it may have had prior and how the long and dangerous shifts of those who usually toil onboard may have played out day by day and week by week. Considerations of offshore labour as a part of the project may well have fallen foul of the commissioning brief of the festival, but there also seems to be a link between the forms of work created by Newsubstance and Skymagic elsewhere that might connect to this choice: their development of drone spectacles.

As noted earlier, Skymagic provided three nights of drone shows to celebrate the opening on *Seemonster* and introduce the work's topical concerns with weather and the climate, recorded on *Seemonster*'s YouTube channel (Seemonster, 2022). The work was a created by Newsubstance's dedicated drone division in collaboration with sound artist Joseph Harris and lighting designers James Bawn and Oliver Suckling. The latter playfully illuminates the former rig in a variety of colours and in rhythm with Harris' mostly electronic soundtrack in ways that often reshapes the extractive structure into abstract forms. Voices of some of Weston's inhabitants are interspersed with the music to comment on the changing weather and winds, the excitement produced by the arrival of Seemonster and finally the need to protect the planet. The drones meanwhile move from constellatory chaos to forming, in turn the logo of *Seemonster*, the rig itself, an umbrella and a sun, a wave, two squawking seagulls, *Seemonster* being lowered into its new home in the bay, the earth, a thank you to Weston and finally the Unboxed logo. At this point the soundtrack features a distinctly professionally trained voice repeating first the work's aims to start conversations about reuse and the British weather followed by 'this was made possible by Unboxed: creativity in the UK'. My own discussion with the security guard about two months after these opening spectacles also revolved around the drones. Might there be another iteration for the closing ceremony? I had heard rumours but was informed that as far as he knew the drones were now in Dubai for use elsewhere. Nevertheless, the opening ceremony's documentation on YouTube highlights the specific aesthetic commitment to create a spectacle devoid of any visible humans. This feature in drone shows is not necessarily unique to *Seemonster*'s opening ceremony but juxtaposed with the installation itself helps draw attention to this disappearance of labour in both the opening spectacle and the installation itself.

As part of his investigation into the logistical mode of artistic production, Shane Boyle surveys a range of projects using drones, notably Amazon's fulfilment centre tours as well as their collaborations with sports, fashion, television and Broadway shows to consider how their deployment serves to 'produce a sense of wonder at what technology can do' (2024: 182). He analyses the ever-deferred promise of a fully automated 'fairy tale' future in declarations by Jeff Bezos and others in which drones will be tasked to undertake the costly 'last mile' logistics of commodity delivery, noting how such professions seek 'to cultivate awe and comfort to encourage the public (and regulators) to keep an open mind as to what else a drone might deliver besides targeted assassinations' (173). Boyle argues, however, that despite their spectacular uses as replacements for either 'unskilled' or 'skilled' human labour – as they come to stand in for warehouse workers in a small selection of fulfilment centres or human performers in Cirque de Soleil shows – drones in fact might both obscure and reveal the replaceability of all workers. Drawing on Sianne Ngai's theorisations of the gimmick, he argues that 'drones operate as gimmicks, not because they lack real-world applications, but because they produce an aesthetic experience of wonder that both obscures and makes visible what they so often propose to replace: human labour' (167–168). Although drones were only a part of *Seemonster* for the opening celebration, it is notable that they are a key aspect of Newsubstance's portfolio, even by another name. I thus contend that Skymagic's drones produced an aesthetic experience of wonder that extends to the absence of representations of work in the installation itself – which in turn can be understood through the concept of the gimmick. As viewers are asked to reflect and move around a self-sustaining energy producing platform – with its own fairy tale reproductions of artificially reproduced weather in the 'cloud portal' and shimmering kinetic scales that glow with the movement of the wind – the labour underpinning both the current destabilised climate or one of the professed routes to fix it disappear. The voiding of human labour from the transition process implies that technology is the sole component that will temper the crisis as teams of scientists and engineers (and sometimes even creative event planners) might magically deploy it towards energetic self-sustenance. In a manner akin to the spectacular magic offered by the opening drone and light show which transformed even the rig itself into a series of flashing abstract shapes, the exploitation and increased precariousness of offshore work is obscured. Whether this work happens to be green or extractive, the historical and contemporary economic imperatives that necessitate it are similarly erased. Additionally, as argued by Boyle, even projects much more radical in their repurposing of capitalist infrastructure carry the risk of attributing counter-logistical power to materials rather than people (2024: 37). Drawing on Bertolt Brecht's discussions of *Umfunktzionierung* (reconfiguration) Boyle continues: 'Whether it is for art or some other context, reconfiguring a circulation technology does not mean severing it from supply chain capitalism and can even entail lending support in new ways' (21). *Seemonster*'s erasure of visible labour manifested in a greened self-sustaining former oil rig demonstrates this point precisely: keeping the messy, dangerous and exploitative working conditions at bay lends support to the lie that technology alone might fix the climate and transcend the need for human labour.

The IPE's explicit championing of the pivotal importance of coal for the historical supremacy of British industry undoubtedly staged extractive labour as a point of pride in a context necessitating high production rates. Yet the mode in which visitors are invited to engage with energy production as they encounter the Hall of Power explicitly places humans as the mediators between nature and technology. *Seemonster* on the other hand gestures towards the necessity of green transition but stages a universe which voids our fossil present from any human hand. This choice thus also counterintuitively lends support to the British state's support for continued North Sea oil extraction as it similarly obfuscates risky and increasingly casualised both extraction and transition labour. This disappearance of human influence on the material conditions that orchestrate climate catastrophe also underpins *About Us*, the final example of Unboxed I will be considering, particularly in its implicit gesturing towards the similarly catastrophic COVID-19 pandemic. Through comparing it with the Sea Travelling Exhibition's disingenuous evocations of Britain's martial and extractive exploits beyond its own borders, my last section will offer a temporally expansive conjunctural analysis to destabilise some disempowering understandings of these crises' histories.

4 Improvement: Land to Outer Space

On a cold January day, I wait for a colleague and friend in the foyer of the recently opened Lightroom, an immersive space developed between 59 Productions, a creative studio offering 'story-based design', and the London theatre company who operates the privately funded Bridge Theatre on the South Bank. Lightroom is nestled at the back of the regenerated creative and commercial quarter erected north of King's Cross station, one of the increasing number of privately owned public spaces popping up across the capital. To the right I glimpse Coal Drop Yards, the former Victorian coal storage and distribution centre, turned into nightclubs during the late 1980s and 1990s heyday of rave culture, before eventually undergoing redevelopment in the late 2000s by the Related Argent group. Long gone are the days of the ubiquitous coal so celebrated in 1951; the whole quarter is now designed to be carbon neutral while the Google headquarters just around the corner showcases the new drivers of progress and industry. My friend and I have come to see 59 Productions' revival of their popular experience *The Moonwalkers*, a narration of lunar expeditions past and present narrated by Tom Hanks. When she joins me, we are eventually ushered into a large and relatively spare room quickly filled with projections across three of its walls as Hanks' voice invites us to partake in his fascination for space exploration. The experience combines archive footage, interviews with past and current astronauts, pointed projections of each female scientist of colour involved in the development of space travel, framed by Hanks' memories of the moon landing alongside extracts of John F Kennedy's 1962 'We chose to go to the Moon' speech. Underpinning the words is a bombastic instrumental soundtrack, occasionally peppered with what I can only describe as non-descript 'world music' voice tracks. My friend immediately notes how the teleological function of the music serves to underline links between the development of human civilisation and space travel. She also points out to what appears to be an eighteenth-century engraving of lovers observing the night sky above a ship at sea in an introductory section projecting historical images of humans looking up to the moon – space exploration becoming an explicit inheritor of earlier European colonial adventures. Shortly before the launch of Lightroom in February 2023, 59 Productions had been one of the key creative organisations behind Unboxed's light and sound installation project *About Us*, which after travelling the country was revived a final time at the Tower of London in November 2022 to close the festival, where I saw it. It is this link to the festival which activated my curiosity to visit *The Moonwalkers*, as *About Us* was similarly grounded in forms of historical narration, and this is a connection that I will revisit as a conclusion to this section. Unexpectedly, however, the image of the eighteenth-century engraving pointed out by my friend helps tie together *The Moonwalker*, *About Us* and my final example from the Festival of Britain: the Sea Travelling Exhibition (STE) housed on the military vessel HMS *Campania*.

The STE was one of the two mobile exhibits held as part of the FOB, travelling more widely across all four nations than its sister land-travelling counterpart. Focusing on this example will continue to widen my analysis of the festival beyond London. More prominently however, I will explore how this exhibit's naval form maps perhaps too neatly onto conceptualisations of Britain as a seafaring nation – with all this implies – extending the focus to the long-standing material effects of colonisation more evidently than the Glasgow exhibition or the Lion and Unicorn Pavilion. The STE's weighted focus on resources and industry as well as Britain's expertise in ships will in turn help me return to the promise of the atomic age underpinning the festival whole. I will then juxtapose the STE's thematic concerns with *About Us* which travelled to Paisley, Derry, Luton and Hull before closing the festival at the Tower of London. *About Us* was billed as 'a live outdoor multimedia display and performance'. It sought to present 'the thematic journey from the Big Bang, to our hyper-connected now' (Outdoor Arts). Projection and moving light technology were used to present 13.8 billion years of history (in 25 minutes), 'lifting the lid on how each and every one of us is an intricate part of the universe' and 'show the magic and wonder of the everyday' (Outdoor Arts 2022: 37). Local choirs singing an original score added an element of live performance to the experience, as did projections of select inhabitants of the visited cities at the end of each show, highlighting the grounded and communal aspect of the event. This was articulated in part as a need to come together after the COVID-19 lockdowns of 2020 and 2021. Both the STE and *About Us* melded temporalities, which beyond the educational and creative purpose of each work also reveal some disavowed political orientations of their discrete periods. The STE's maritime setting formally and thematically linked imperial conquest to space exploration and the promise of the coming atomic age, the latter undermined by the HMS *Campania*'s near-immediate redeployment as the flag carrier for Britain's first nuclear bomb tests. Meanwhile *About Us*' juxtaposition of choral singing and the all-encompassing motif of the network linking past, present and future worked to render these categories inconsequential. Both events glossed over violences, whether gone-by or yet to come. *About Us* in fact erased the importance of human history all together in its assessment our current crises.

4.1 A Nation of Seafarers

The exhibition presented on the *Campania* in large parts duplicates in miniature several aspects of the South Bank exhibits, although the rationale for using a ship to represent the British nation to itself is particularly stressed. Starting her voyage in Southampton, the HMS *Campania* travelled to all nations of Britain and to the North of Ireland. A hugely popular exhibit across all its stopovers, the long white aircraft carrier was temporarily refitted and adorned with a large 'Festival of Britain' inscription across its side. It is organised across three successive themes – 'The Land of Britain', 'Discovery' and 'The People at Home'. The exhibition thus links the local and the domestic to Britain's global reach, linking its insular identity to an expansive sense of space, mirroring the link between the present and the long sense of the past diagnosed by Conekin. Most of the exhibits are displayed on two lower floors of the ship's hangar although visitors can enjoy a small boat exhibition and access a refreshment counter on the top deck. Entering the ship on the lowest deck, visitors are first introduced to a small geological section on the origins of the island, before passing a compressed section on coal, steel and industry which despite not fully replicating a mine includes a somewhat immersive black corridor featuring mining gear stuck to its walls. As in Glasgow, strong emphasis is placed on the development of coal, steam and industry with an extended discussion of their relationship to Britain's impact on world development. Most of what subsequently follows is heavily focused on transport – with an expected emphasis on ships and British achievements in technology and their benefit to the world. As the catalogue states: 'It is no accident that this particular version of the South Bank story should be housed on a ship – indeed what better setting could be found for the story of a nation that lives on the sea and by it?' (STE Catalogue, 1951: 8) Alongside jet engines, model cars, traffic lights and airplanes, visitors can look upon early navigation maps and contemporary mechanised navigation aids as well as panels explaining the inner functioning of large ships such as the *Campania*. The overall presentation of this section's title above the displays on the wall contains elements of space age design, showing a three-dimensional

Empire, Extraction and Power 55

model of the *Campania* trailed by clean, curved lines against the backdrop of a thin spiral.

The following section moves onto industry, featuring a relief map of Britain and the North of Ireland on the ship floor pinpointing the main industrial centres, products and locations of production. Visitors can also interact with different objects of industrial design, such as self-priming centrifugal pumps or smaller objects such as thermometers displayed in hexagonal shelves against the walls. The exhibition then continues to a section exploring 'the living world', centred around Charles Darwin and biology, and featuring models of gulls and gull's nests illustrating animal behaviour. Next is the dedicated outer space display which I will discuss further down, before the journey takes visitors to the upper deck and then back below for the final sections focused on 'the rural scene', 'health' and finally 'homes and gardens', 'the seaside' and 'Great Britons'. Homes and Gardens is another opportunity to engage in British design, this time focused on domestic gadgets and interiors featuring amongst many other objects, figurines of Alice in Wonderland and assorted characters as well as miniature teapots and cups, reminiscent of the Lion and Unicorn's section on eccentricity. Just before the exit, the final section gives visitors the opportunity to salute some of the men who have added to Britain's great maritime tradition, such as Raleigh, Drake or James Cook, celebrated as the 'greatest of them all' (STE Catalogue, 1951: 31).

The catalogue also overall reveals itself to be perhaps the most candid record of the FOB regarding the role of Britain's seafaring ventures such as Cook's and their implications for global reach and resource extraction. While empire is not explicitly named, the relationship between naval prowess, imperialism and current economic and geopolitical status is straightforwardly pointed to. Here the statement that without the enterprise of ship owners the growth of the Commonwealth would have followed a different path is replicated. The entry further notes how 'The development of the world's sea trade also has been largely led by British enterprise, fed by British capital and served by British technical and engineering skill ... Without a mercantile marine such as we have now, we people of Britain and our industries would starve' (STE Catalogue, 1951: 17). Further along, in a section on 'The Earth' focused on the development of geological surveys, the extractive purpose of British enterprise becomes even more blatant:

> Britain created the first geological survey, and showed the world how valuable this science can be when it is organised for the service and development of whole countries. Without it, recovery of the Earth's hidden riches – coal, oil, minerals and the rest – would still be a very haphazard affair. (STE Catalogue, 1951: 21)

These mentions of extraction in the descriptions make Britain's imperial mission more explicit than those of the Lion and Unicorn Pavilion or the Industrial Power Exhibition: British capital is served by technical engineering skills to develop maritime technology without which British industry would starve. This industry in turn is enabled by the ability to uncover and map fossil fuels and minerals beyond the celebrated British coal fields, which alongside steam enables the machine age to generate more capital. Despite the period's anxieties pertaining to the detonating of atomic bombs in Hiroshima and Nagasaki, optimism for the coming nuclear age is both evident and embedded within the lineage of British scientific developments, following in this case Glasgow's itinerary. Although there is no dedicated space to nuclear technology, the section of the ship dedicated to Power does gesture to its promise, as noted in the catalogue: 'The harnessing of STEAM was one of the really great events in the history of civilisation. It was then that man (sic) first came to possess a power greater than that of the horse. Possibly we are now on the threshold of another such great achievement – control of the power in the atom's nucleus' (STE Catalogue, 1951: 14). The placing of these displays on a temporarily decommissioned military ship further emphasises martial aspects of Britain's imperial history, and as I shall argue, eventually destabilises the peaceful atomic promise presented in the festival.

Here I would like to draw on Andreas Malm again in his study of an engraving depicting the British 1837 discovery of coal on the Malaysian island of Labuan he describes as an 'Urbild' of the fossil economy. The image depicts two white men, one wearing a Royal Navy uniform and the other excitedly gesticulating at the seam. Malm writes that the scene exudes a sense of mastery and proprietary rights, registering the moment when foreign shores are integrated into the fossil economy, 'an economy of self-sustaining growth predicated on the growing consumption of fossil fuels and therefore generating a sustained growth in CO_2 emissions' (Malm, 2017: 19). Malm stresses how the expansion of empire is predicated on extraction, even if his conclusions regarding the consequences of this invention are resolutely less optimistic than those drawn in 1951. Indeed one might see a direct line between the function of the geological survey and the image presented by Malm. While the first state-sponsored survey of Great Britain was conducted in 1835, it was enabled by earlier privately funded surveys in Europe but also Eastern Jamaica. The latter were conducted by plantation (and slave) owner Thomas de La Beche in 1827, who later financially supported the 1835 survey of Devon as part of the subsequent mapping of British resources and became the first director of the Ordnance Geological Survey (Geological Survey). Thus, British science and technology were enabled by access to and experiments in colonised lands and slave plantations, which were in turn deployed to aid extraction be it mineral, or, as I will argue, agricultural.

The links between the development of state-sponsored scientific innovations and improvements in relationship to empire brings me back to some of the overarching questions underpinning my exploration. Malm's frank, if not singular, elaborations on imperialism's development of extractivist technologies also helps clarify their relationship to the expansion of global capitalism:

> British imperialists came to Labuan with a clear goal in mind: to find coal ... More precisely, we can, judging from the lithograph, surmise that the entrepreneur present at the scene hoped to earn money, while the officer saw in the deposits a prop for the steamboat lines in the area. Such profoundly intentional enterprises were anything but spectacular: rather they were trivially typical for the merchant and the mariner trying to reproduce themselves at the time and, if possible, expand their own empires. (Malm, 2017: 70)

Placing reduced segments of the key larger exhibits of the FOB on the HMS *Campania* highlights this relationship between the merchant and the mariner. Just as Malm notes that in 1837 they are not joined in some benevolent scientific mission, so the 1951 ship can also draw our attention to how the FOB not only euphemistically conjures Britain's colonial history as one of progress but also its leading role in the development of a capitalist world system emerging through its theories and practices of agriculture.

4.2 Agricultural Improvement

Extraction of fossil fuels and minerals underpin many British imperial ventures in conjunction with the development of modern industry since the late eighteenth century as highlighted by Malm. However, the earlier appropriation of land across the globe from the fifteenth century onwards was also predicated on developments in agricultural production, driving the expansion of plantations in neighbouring Ireland all the way to the distant Americas by a belief in Britain's distinct prowess in matters of farming. This agricultural expertise is hinted at from the start of the STE, and directly linked to a similar ability to discover and mine minerals: 'Forebears developed 'the most diversely and efficiently farmed countryside in the world' ... By now we have exhausted our supply of some minerals; but even here the knowledge gained in their working has not been lost for we have applied it to new deposits overseas' (STE Catalogue: 11). In a later section on 'The Land', great explorers are celebrated for their propensity to journey and return to the most 'extravagant' or 'severe' places, leading to 'exploration, and exploration to development of the land by using those skills we learned at home' (STE Catalogue: 18).

The specific development of these agricultural skills is key to Ellen Meiksins Wood's discussion of the agrarian roots of capitalism in early modern England. Her work is an effort to challenge the naturalisation of capitalism presented in what she names the 'commercialisation model' of history which argues that capitalism emerges straightforwardly out of earlier mercantile social forms and is propelled into being by the Industrial Revolution. She defines capitalism as

> the dominant mode of appropriation based on the complete dispossession of direct producers who (unlike chattel slaves) are legally free and whose surplus labour is appropriated by purely 'economic means.' Because direct producers in a fully developed capitalism are propertyless, and because their only access to the means of production, to their requirements of their own reproduction, even to the means of their own labour, is the sale of their labour power in exchange for a wage, capitalists can appropriate the workers' surplus labour without direct coercion. (1999: 96)

In Meiksins Wood's account, this system's early origins emerge in the English countryside and develop due to two interlinked factors. The first was an early centralisation of the state and its appropriation of the role of protector leading to much less 'extra-economic' (i.e. coercion by force) power being in the hands of the parcelised feudal ruling class as in other parts of Europe. The second was the disproportionate amount of land held by much fewer landlords, leading the land to be worked by tenants. Thus, she argues that in this context agrarian landlords had a strong incentive to encourage or where possible compel their tenants to reduce costs by increasing productivity (99–100). She then further traces how these practices develop alongside political and economic theories of 'improvement'. These theories will eventually severely impact not only Britain, but the world as a whole and with long and far-reaching consequences.

'Improvement' here refers to the imperative to increase labour and land productivity, finding ever more efficient ways of rendering the land profitable for landlords, igniting legal and technological changes underpinned by the need for increased profit. This conception of improvement is most prominently found in the works of John Locke, philosopher and investor in the Royal Africa Company, particularly in his thoughts on property. Meiksins Wood notes that the 'theme running throughout his discussion is that the earth is there to be made productive and profitable, and that is why private property, which emanates from labour, trumps common possession' (110). European colonial projects can be read in the first instance as processes of enclosure, and many imperialist ideologies took the lack of formalised or recognisable land ownership structures as a justification of these lands' violent appropriation. Yet Locke's theories of improvement, as applied in his case to the Americas, had additional consequences. As Meiksins Wood argues, theories of 'improvement' imply that by the standards of English agrarian capitalism occupancy alone is not enough to establish property rights and constitutes insufficiently profitable agriculture as waste. As she writes: 'This redefinition of occupancy and waste means that land in America is open to colonisation because an acre of land in 'unimproved' America has not produced exchange value comparable to that of improved land in England' (1999: 158). Through this logic colonisers become creators of value and are thus not figured as expropriators of local populations but as 'improvers' adding to the common good, characterised by the formalisation of a capitalist political economy.

The STE's spatial organisation performs this Lockean narrative across many of its sections, where a specific British genius for efficiency and productivity is performed again and again not only in agriculture, but also mining, transport and of course seafaring. This lays the ground for a logic of capitalist accumulation which will eventually come to structure the world via imperial conquest. A common hunger for resources certainly drove earlier European colonial ventures and pre-existing intercontinental trade networks undoubtedly enabled the exchange of their spoils acquired through chattel slavery and other violent modes of coercion. Yet it was the eventual supremacy of British imperialism from the late seventeenth century onwards which sparked and extended England's capitalist logic. As Meiksins Wood argues, what was distinctive about this new form of appropriation was a system of coercions of its own, *economic* imperatives, reinforcing and eventually capable of replacing political domination by the compulsion to engage in the capitalist market and its attendant social relations (165). Although in 1951 Britain's days of direct global reach were now numbered, the short section on Outer Space also seems to indicate that new opportunities never cease to be on the horizon to still improve elsewhere, this British spirit encapsulated in the exhibition's closing slogan: Endeavour, Resolution, Adventure, Discovery (31). As such, the displays on the HMS *Campania* draw attention to yet also gloss over how imperial adventures are fundamental not only to the continuation of capitalism but to its expansion on a global scale.

As a final point on the FOB's contradictory messaging, I will now return to its evocations of the atom on the ship and elsewhere as a contemporaneous example of how discourses of British technological progress obfuscate aspects of this progress' continued violent interventions in and need for overseas spaces. Hornsey notes the structuring motif of the atom throughout the festival, not only in dedicated displays but also in patterns produced on carpets, furnishings and household objects 'derived from atomic crystallography' (2010: 69) His discussion points to two contrasting visions circulating at the time, one of optimism for scientific and aesthetic enlightenment offered for example by the festival's design choices, and the other grounded in the threat of mass annihilation recently witnessed in Japan and heightened by the Cold War context. Comparing a Pathé newsreel showing how a nuclear blast had branded a pattern into a woman's flesh with one of the FOB atom-based textile designs, he writes that 'a brand-new pattern for a woman's dress became the celebrated alternative to its disavowed other: a dress pattern branded into a woman's flesh' (69–70). This ambivalence was also at the heart of the British government's stated attitudes to nuclear technology. As Hornsey argues, the concerted efforts made to teach an uncertain British public about the science behind this strange and terrible new force 'repeatedly contrasted two future scenarios, whereby the social benefits of nuclear energy were cautiously foregrounded against the foreboding possibility of global apocalypse' (69). Overall, emphasis was put on the environmentally structuring function of the atom, creating 'a very specific understanding of how a certain structure of time, space, and circuitous repetition inherently underpinned the stability of the material world' (72). Yet these visions of a brave new future which would harness the atom to propel Britain – and through this the word – into a harmonious age of possibilities contrasted with the mostly secretive scientific work undertaken since the decision to develop the country's first atomic bomb on 8 January 1947.

As Britain was locked out of cooperating with the United States following President Harry Truman's decision to withhold his country's nuclear knowledge in 1946, Britain went against its ally in making the decision to pursue atomic energy, both civilian and military. In a move informed by the increasing tensions between the USSR and its former wartime allies, Britain set up its first Atomic Weapons Research Establishment in Aldermaston in 1950 (Bennett, 2022). The decision to go ahead with Britain's first nuclear tests was made in May 1951. While the choice of location for these first tests was not settled until after the Conservative election win of October 1951, the transportation logistics for the detonation of the first plutonium bomb on Australia's Montebello islands the following year were already being determined – the flag carrier chosen being the HMS *Campania* herself. As with many other festival elements, proposals were made by the festival committee to extend the STE's lifespan, in this case a proposal to have the ship visit other Commonwealth countries. As this idea was proposed to the government by Secretary of Foreign Affairs, Patrick Gordon Walker, a reply from then Secretary of the Admiralty and future Prime Minister James Callaghan came on the 22nd of May, stating: '. . . we expect to know definitely within the next month or so whether the particular job we had in mind for her is likely to materialise. If it does, and the chances are it will, I am afraid that we should not be able to release her' (1951). This fact was finally confirmed on 3 July. And so, just after a year after the festival's closure, the *Campania* moored to the West of its former Australian colony, and shortly thereafter the vison of the peaceful atomic future morphed into the obliterating promise of the nuclear cold war. Atoms also structured a large part of 2022's *About Us* as part of their recursive network motif which retracted and expanded from the micro-organism all the way to the galactic scale of the Milky Way. Presented more as agent than an agent of progress, here too the representation of the atom is folded into a problematic historical narration – albeit for different, if not unrelated, reasons to 1951.

4.3 Amoebas and Assembly Lines

I will now shift my attention to *About Us*, showcased in Paisley, Derry, Caernarfon, Luton, Hull and finally London – seventy-one years after the *Campania*'s final stint as an exhibition space in Glasgow. Despite the direct link made by Theresa May between both festivals, the purpose of Unboxed 2022 was less grounded in representing the nation to itself but rather to showcase Britain's creativity to itself. Thus the mode of presentation and deployment of technology for this event, as with other projects in the festival, would have eschewed the more conventional presentational/educational mode of the exhibition more typical of a museum or of most the FOB's offerings. A collaboration between 59 productions, the Poetry society and The Stemmettes – an organisation encouraging women and non-binary participation in science – this touring event combined 'multimedia installations with animation, poetry, original music and live performance to explore the myriad connections between us, our planet, and the wider cosmos' (59 Productions). This event thus blends visual elements with multivocal voiceovers offering forms of poetic commentary on the moving images. Additionally, voices from a choir located on a platform to the left of the projection area intermittently swell over the recorded soundtrack, punctuating the distinct emotional states of the work. These moving images skilfully adapt to the diverse backdrops through projection mapping, appearing on facades as diverse as Hull's 1930s-style Town Hall, Paisley abbey, Caernarfon's castle or the Tower of London where I saw it in November 2022. Before the event starts the following words are projected on the building's ramparts for spectators to read: 'This stone was once a forest, listen quietly and you may hear her dream about the birds in her hair.' This line it turns out sets the scene for what is to come, gesturing to a recursive relationship between physics, the natural world, humanity and technology, linked by the overarching image of the network.

Then, a soft Scottish woman's voice announces the probable start of the event in two minutes, quoting Albert Einstein to inform us that 'the distinction between past, present and future is a stubbornly persistent illusion' and at this point the show properly begins. *About Us* begins with what is a rather familiar narration of earth's creation starting with the fusing of atomic particles – which we are told we are all but temporary constellations of – to water and amoebas, and jellyfish. As projected trees adorn the relief of the Tower, a certain emphasis is placed on bacteria and how our bodies 'are stomping grounds for invisible life' and 'that this life that air b'n bs withs us', the voiceover further noting 'that there is no boundary between me and this flesh mob'. A certain emphasis is placed on visualising interconnections through presenting merging and splitting cells, DNA helixes or plants stems sprouting to grow horizontally. The projected forest morphs into dinosaurs and whales while the choir ominously sings 'all is changing'. As mammals and insects start to appear, the anticipatory feel of the singing and composition rises until the sound becomes fully rhythmic, and fragments of voices speaking English and Welsh are heard – humanity has now joined this cosmic whole. On the tower's ramparts human figures explode into hieroglyphs and alphabets, and for a short moment the walls of the Tower of London resemble an Ancient Egyptian temple. This now fully signals the rise of human civilisation and its attendant expression in language and culture. The music becomes increasingly electronic as the show accelerates human history, as visions of high rises, city maps, container ships and assembly lines start flashing up. The interconnected network here again serves as a strong visual motif with motorways driving into each other or mass manufactured goods merging across the façade and the voiceover evokes 'indigenous rainforests funnelled into factories, sweatshops, mines'. At this point the projection loops back to earlier images of tree roots which become superimposed and then replaced by motherboards, which in turn get replaced by rhizomatic patterns emerging below forests. This is where the network as an underlying concept is most stressed, as the voiceover declares: 'were there enough networks of rhizomes would glow phosphorescent in the soil. We're here too, underground, lit not by glowing roots but by a vast jungle of fiber-optics'. Subsequently a rising musical crescendo begins as we return to images of army tanks, mechanised agriculture, nurses wearing face masks, medical pills on production lines and finally forest fires, hinting at imminent catastrophe. Suddenly the light goes off, and as the choir now gently sings 'we are thirty-two trillion cells', glittering DNA helixes briefly reconstitute photographs of human individuals who quickly dissolve back into atoms, replaced by images of growing flowers which are in turn replaced by projections resembling the initial representations of galaxies and outer space. The work ends with the contours of the Tower of London being traced around what appears to be many trails of drifting stars.

Despite the rejection of history implied in the opening Einstein quote and reaffirmed just minutes later in the assertion that *About Us* is not 'a story about the universe, science or history', this event needs to be both historically analysed as well as critiqued for its stated denial of history. My latter point rests on the deployment of the network as a frame but also links to my former reading of *About Us* as in fact being an exemplary manifestation of specific historic anxieties which emerged over the COVID-19 pandemic. The documentation video of the process created by 59 Productions confirms how much the virus affected the creators' thinking. Executive director Rebecca Collis highlights how difficult it had been execute the project over the pandemic, and *About Us* was always 'meant to be a celebration ... something that brought people and communities back together after being isolated for so long' (Unboxed, 2022). This sentiment is also echoed by an unnamed choir member who rejoices in the opportunity to sing again after two years and that it was 'just an amazing experience to come back together and be part of something' (Unboxed, 2022). The importance of the network motif is made insistently clear by the creative director Lysander Ashton, who states that 'connection was important from the beginning, networks macro to micro, to the cosmic through to nature though infrastructure and technology, networks really surround and join us. Especially nature, we are all part of the same system and we've all come from the same place' (Unboxed, 2022). The inclusion of live human choirs against this backdrop is also particularly stressed. Project composer Nithin Sawhney observes that 'human voices are powerful and empathic' and they can humanise something that may feel quite abstract, so that everyone can feel something and really relate to what's going on' (Unboxed, 2022). Thus the choirs enable the work to move representation of interconnectivity to the production of such interconnectivity in the moment of performance through the use of vocal choral togetherness.

While never explicitly named in the performance, many elements also gesture – purposefully or not – towards ideas of contagion and its overcoming in the two years prior to the stagings of *About Us*, underpinned by the expressed need for togetherness following the COVID-19 mitigation lockdowns. Most obviously perhaps, the projected images of nurses and medicine presented alongside forest fires towards the end hint a sense of catastrophe before the light show dissolves back into the vastness of space. Alongside these images, the deployment of choirs also hints at the pandemic – both as a symbol of existence under lockdowns as well as the alleged collective victory over COVID-19. Choirs, alongside indoor performances and certain types of indoor sports were one of the most affected forms of expressions and entertainment by the restrictions on communal gatherings enforced by states worldwide to mitigate contagion. The transmission vectors of the SARS Cov2 virus meant choirs were broadly banned from practicing for about eighteen months in their full and usual in person capacity. In a review of the scientific rationales for the shutting down of choirs, Kay Norton notes that like vigorous cheering and chanting, singing propels plumes of exhaled droplets and aerosols which are easily inhaled, which is further enhanced by the velocity added by the articulation of text, projection of vocal sound, high-energy (loud) vocalisation, and whispered or breathy tones (2024: 64). Indeed, choirs more so than theatre events or sports made the news as emblematically risky, whether practiced at religious services (Read, 2020) or as a form of creative expression (McKie, 2020). This extensive ban was bemoaned on two specific grounds. The first noted the benefits of choral singing as a remedy against social isolation in general and measuring the practice's specific health benefits against the stated risks of high transmissibility. The second objection drew on a general perception of choirs as a horizontally organised mode of creative expression and through this their community building or enhancing properties, especially amateur collective singing.

Choral singing is often constructed and promoted as a social and individual good. A cursory google search for 'benefits of choirs' brings up a plethora of articles citing scientific research on the cognitive and bonding functions of collective singing, from sources ranging from the liberal *Guardian* to the hard right *Daily Telegraph* (Shaikh, 2020; Sample, 2023). Community music scholarship also often takes these benefits as a starting point, although also often applies these benefits to social cohesion more broadly. For example, in the most recent *Oxford Handbook of Community Singing* published 2024, one of many sections outlining both individual and social well-being of community singing, Kayla Drudge and Anna E. Nekola argue that 'the intersection of the radical transformation of music through a mission of community-building and the radical transformation of community-building through music points us to the power of imagining both, music *and* community, in new and multiple ways' (371). Furthermore, central to this transformative potential are conceptions of participation and (artistic) citizenship, which in some cases also directly draw from similar arguments made in theatre studies as they apply to the political functions of the Greek chorus. David Elliott and Marissa Silverman argue that enacting progressive change 'through 'talk-talk-talk' is not enough: physical, musical, and emotional participation is required' (2018: 373). This understanding of choirs is also implicit in Nitin Sawhney's pronouncements on the use of choirs in *About Us* as he stresses the emotionally connective power of deploying the human voice, so that *everyone* can feel and relate to as large an abstraction as a journey from 'the big bang to our hyperconnected now'. Choral singing in this context becomes a metonym for society under lockdown, as isolated voices first rejoin each other via Zoom before signalling in their physical co-presence eighteen months later that collectively 'we' have overcome the virus.

Additionally, the connectivity which enables everyone to feel and relate also gestures to the other primary stated concern of the work, the fundamentally networked basis of human existence.

4.4 Death Comes to Town

Alongside Ashton, *About Us*' senior video designer Nicol Scott similarly asserts that the design was founded on the concept of networks 'from macro to micro, cosmic to nature to infrastructure' (Unboxed, 2022). My experience of the whole performance's mise-en-scène confirms that this was a recognisable feature, as atoms from space transform into jellyfish and tree roots into fibre-optic cables, and the voiceover reminds us how our bodies are made and support other forms of bacterial life. The visual and aural representation of infinite interlinked techno-eco-human networks thus both dilutes and flattens a general crisis of which COVID was at the time the most memorable manifestation. Insofar as a certain interdependence between nature and humanity is evident – we all need to eat and drink after all – the management of this interdependence is historically constituted. For example, while viruses are indeed part of the ecosystems we inhabit and for which our bodies are evidently permeable receptacles, our vulnerabilities to and management of viruses in the current moment are to a large degree the result of human activity.

In this regard, returning to my earlier discussion of Meiksins Wood on the agrarian origins of capitalism offers a useful way of considering the role of human activity in the proliferation, contagiousness and management of viruses. Tracing the role of agriculture not only for the development of capitalism but also for its more recent reconfiguration of nature is in this case illuminating. While Meiksins Wood convincingly locates the origins of capitalism in the English countryside, it is notable, as Søren Mau notes, that the real subsumption of agriculture only accelerated in the latter part of the twentieth century (2023: 258). Mau identifies three key processes: technological changes in the form of mechanisation, fertilisers and biotechnological manipulation; restructuring and new divisions of labour; and an ever-tighter subjection of agriculture to market forces (261). The ecological destruction driven by the shifts towards agribusiness also drove a global expansion of expropriative practices. This has led to the global displacement of surplus rural populations into the ever-growing urban slums of the global South (271). It is exactly these factors that Mike Davis identified as key to the dizzying emergence and spread of SARS-Cov2, the virus that kept many of us physically apart between 2020 and 2021. In his sobering 2005 diagnosis of the threat of avian flu, *The Monster at our Door*, and in his introduction to its timely 2020 re-release, Davis stresses the undeniable link between agri-business, poverty and the multiplication of deadly respiratory viruses over the past 30 years in general – and in the new edition the advent of SARS-Cov2 in particular. Davis' diagnosis points to globalised capitalism and its need to valorise of as many spheres of activity as possible, including health care as stressed by the lack of investment in vaccines due to profitability concerns. The origins and rapid mutations and proliferation of new viruses are also direct consequences of the development of an improved agriculture, located in contemporary practices of agri-business. Davis thus usefully draws our focus away from the supposed transhistorical ubiquity of pandemics as simply 'natural'. In his analysis, the most integral aspects leading to the possibilities of new viruses are: human to animal contact linked to deforestation itself linked to increased cattle farming, the cramped conditions of chicken factories and cover-ups of sudden deadly bird-flu epidemics to maintain profit rates, and the similarly cramped conditions of mega slums where the already endemic lack of healthcare and unavoidable physical closeness facilitate not only easy contagion but also the mutations that can make each new strain more resistant to immunity than the next (Davis, 2020).

Meiksins Wood's project is one seeking to understand the specific historical origins of capitalism in socio-historical factors without falling back on determinist arguments that would locate its rise to hegemony in earlier mercantile forms of trade. Through this she usefully draws attention away from the more commonly held understanding of capitalism as co-emergent with technologies of the industrial revolution, instead refocusing on the specific role of human labour and its role in value production. The move performed by evocations of the network as presented in *About Us* becomes in this regard even more problematic; viewers are warned of the dangers of industrial production and ecological disaster, but the recurring and recursive motif of the network which links galactic matter to the internet and assembly lines also implies a certain inevitability in this situation. For all the similar molecular composition of the diverse bodies projected in *About Us*' finale, the felt realities of the catastrophe briefly hinted at in this project cannot be understood to be equally distributed whether in time or space, even as the – distinctly human – temporalities manifested by any focus on ecological destruction inevitably crash into each other. Indeed, as Malm also argues in *Fossil Capital*, 'in an elevated sense of the term, every conjuncture now combines relics and arrows, loops and postponements that stretch from the deepest past to the most distant future' (2016: 8). Some of the origins of our current conjectures might by now feel so distant – as the early modern period does – that they have become naturalised.

In this the seductive image of networks can come to stand in as a handy explanation for an overwhelming present where mastery of nature feels like a minimal factor in the face of a physical environment that can otherwise destroy us. As is evident in their visual quality, networks operate through a flattened form – favouring a spatial approach to apprehending social existence, determined by a multiplicity of connections and interactions determined horizontally across human and non-human forms. As explored in my description of *About Us*, these linkages were foregrounded, both in poetic mentions of our bodies' enmeshment with bacteria or projected images connecting DNA to tree roots to fibre-optic cables. Seb Franklin notes how the popularity of networks as a theoretical model for reading texts and contexts elides 'the historical dynamics and ongoing processes of capitalist accumulation' – these historical and ongoing processes being for example exemplified in the relationship between a specific form of English colonial conquest, accumulation and agriculture (2016). The focus on outward manifestations of production and reproduction afforded by the spatial metaphor of the network thus 'occludes the conceptual schema underlying the violent abstractions of not only the commodity and the wage relation, but also race, gender, sexuality, and nationality amongst many more' that are imbricated with capitalist accumulation' (2016) Through conjuring the network, *About Us*' obfuscates Britain's fundamental role in the empire driven development of the fossil economy all while highlighting both this historical moment's ongoing manifestations (globalised logistics and manufacturing) and devastating effects (forest fires). Of course no British public art project given the brief to be 'open, original and optimistic' would realistically present viewers with the relatively complex intricacies of Britain's original role in enabling the current scale of the climate crisis through its imperial exploits and fossil fuel driven development of global capitalism; yet a state-funded project predicated on showcasing 'Creativity in the UK' and which fully diffuses the exact historical and geographical processes and locations of the origins of such a crisis also runs the risk of, at best, inadvertently presenting itself as both an innovator in solving such a crisis and thus absolved of any implication in its creation. At worst, it can be read as a nihilistic acceptance as the sheer scale of networks and interconnections rids humanity of history tout-court, and through this any belief in the human-driven possibility of large-scale social change.

Jo Littler offers an incisive reading of how images of the coming space age and Britain's involvement in it at the FOB can be directly linked back to earlier imperial imaginaries. She argues that 'Imperial expansionism continued to be validated through and to symbolically reside in science, and attempts to find new places to be known, possessed and mapped marked the perpetuation of imperial narratives of discovery'. Drawing on Nicholas Dirk she points to how cartography and science, in practicing surveying and mapping in order to posses, were all colonial enterprises. Thus, she states that 'Imperial mapping is extended in and through scientific discovery: British imperial expansion on the earth naturally progresses into the exploration of space' (27). This natural progression is also hinted at in *The Moonwalkers*, 59 Productions' immersive experience briefly discussed in the opening of this section, linking space travel to eighteenth-century seafaring ventures. The language used during the work and replicated in the programme also echo earlier imperial discourses, traces of which were also to be found in the STE's catalogue. Planetary Physicist Shannon Curry notes for example that the moon's South Pole may be the repository of water and other, unnamed 'precious resources' which could be used for the establishment of lunar bases and further explorations (The Moonwalkers: 39) Great stress is placed throughout the show on the necessity to reignite space exploration as this 'might be our best hope for solving our challenges on earth' (The Moonwalkers: 15) While it is now all of humanity that is appealed to in this renewed need to extend human adventures into space – women and people of colour's historical and present participation is particularly stressed in the footage – the underlying logics of surveying, extraction and possession of new frontiers remain as strong as in 1951.

Moreover, *The Moonwalkers* performs a similar obscuring of history as *About Us*. Although Kennedy's speech and subsequent international tour is central, emphasis is placed on the inclusive 'we' apparently used by audiences of the president's speech, as American achievements come to stand in for humanity's progress. The US' early success in reaching the moon is framed throughout as a benefit to all humankind and testament to a new dawn of peaceful global scientific progress, with not a single mention of the Cold War's role in propelling both America and the USSR into space – the latter in fact first. Indeed, *The Moonwalkers* contains hardly any mention of the USSR, despite a small homage to Cosmonauts towards the end of the experience, and the catalogue mentions the word Soviet once, euphemistically noting that in 1969 'only two nations (*sic*) had the technology to reach other worlds' (The Moonwalkers: 13). I point this out not because of some desire to rehabilitate the USSR's similarly path-breaking role in the development of space travel. Rather, I wish to point to how very specific human and material reasons such as resource extraction and geopolitical conflict between hegemonic power blocks are fundamental in the development of this technology, and its consequences for all humankind.

At the 2019 London Historical Materialism conference, which focused on disaster communism and extinction capitalism, Ruthie Wilson Gilmore commented that for many people across the world, extinction had occurred some centuries ago, that catastrophes have already happened (Wilson-Gilmore, 2019). Although the post-war enthusiasm presented in 1951 does involuntarily locate the origins of this catastrophe more clearly than About Us' 'thematic journey from the Big Bang, to our hyper-connected now', these catastrophes had, of course, already happened in 1951. They were to continue happening as the refitted HMS *Campania* sailed to the Monte Bello islands in Northern Australia in 1952 to conduct Britain's first nuclear tests and continue in 2025 as NASA and Elon Musk's SpaceX are about to respectively launch their new rockets towards the moon's surface while down here on earth many have to endure floods and droughts.

5 Conclusion

I began this Element proposing to take a conjunctural approach to analyse interconnections between two generously state-funded festivals celebrating British national culture, exploring these festivals' relationship to the state – and through this questions of empire, power and extraction. This is an approach I maintained, especially in my second section's diagnosis of the development of the legal apparatus which very concretely constructed Britain as a bounded and increasingly hermetic territory. Similarly, it is specific state practices which allow space exploration and the development of nuclear weaponry. It is also still the state which regulates legislations regarding resource extraction, taxation and labour laws. I expanded my temporal frame of analysis in my final section, stressing the specific rural origin of this socio-economic context which restructured the world through subsequent imperial conquests, in terms not only of power but the development of agriculture based on the production of value. This is where the longue durée underpinning our epochal conjuncture most prominently came to the fore, as the long-reaching consequences of seventeenth-century theories of agricultural improvement rippled through the world in the form of a novel virus. The 'post' pandemic environment which heavily influenced the themes and form of *About Us* is also deeply marked by ecological disaster, which, as Malm writes, 'stretches from the deepest past to the most distant future' (2016: 8). Climate was not elided in *About Us*, but in approaching catastrophe through the spatial metaphor of the network disappeared the very historical – and thus human – causes of its existence. As Malm remarks, it is undeniable that 'space is a crucial dimension' for apprehending ecological crises, but that the 'spaces of climate change are relevant insofar as they are folded within the process: the change, the warming. As the word indicates this tempest is eminently temporal' (11–12). Following from Malm's assertion, approaching this current moment of general crisis through apprehending both longer and shorter temporal processes structuring the present is vital. My effort to do so was to explore how the historic moment of social democracy in Britain might help us understand a very recent past often understood as an accelerated unravelling of said social democracy.

Given the ongoing centrality of Margaret Thatcher's 1979 election to the conception of Britain's economic shifts up to this day, characterised by privatisation, market liberalisation and the gradual rupturing of the social democratic compact, these two historical periods are often approached in opposition rather than in conjunction with one another. This opposition is most evident in my comparison between the IPE and *Seemonster* which moves from state ownership of extractive infrastructures in 1951 to a contemporary economy predicated on outsourced labour, privatisation and rentier capitalism. Yet nostalgic discourses that surround the social-democratic era of the 1950s can often elide its inherent problems as well as obscure how some of these problems set the scene for or perdure in our contemporary moment. Gurminder Bhambra uncovers how not only resource extraction but also systems of taxation in the colonies underpinned welfare programmes in Britain. This included a scheme proposed by John Maynard Keynes to let prices rise more than real wages to raise funds for the Second World War, rejected as too regressive for the British nation itself but implemented in India, leading to the 1943 Bengal famine (2022). Her work illuminates the additional imperial foundations enabling the British state to roll out generous national welfare programmes during the war and the years following it. Many activists and scholars, including Richard Hornsey, have also drawn attention to the sexist, heteronormative and white supremacist imaginaries that underpin the big reforms and planning of the period, and this is a part of what Toscano points to when he notes late fascism's harking back to a time of Big Capital and Big Labour (9). As explored through Koram and El-Enany's work in my section dealing with The Lion and Unicorn Pavilion and *Story-Trails*, the post-war Labour Party was also deeply invested in cementing the concept of and eventually fixing the boundaries the British nation.

My initial curiosity towards Unboxed as a comparative object of analysis was driven by an interest in investigating why a Conservative PM would choose to inject such a large amount of money into a festival explicitly drawing from a famous social-democratic predecessor. Yet in excavating the broader geopolitical and social context of the Festival of Britain enabled me to more fully grasp how many of its aspects, prominently nationalism, technology and disavowed imperial conceptions of the British state are easily mutable across economic systems. In this regard, the 2024 return of a Labour government to power offers an additional opportunity to reflect on conclusions drawn in separate sections of this Element. Ostensibly self-defined as a centre-left party, its policies on welfare have not presented a radical break from those of their Conservative predecessors, with cuts to disability benefits framed by similar moralising statements regarding welfare dependency and the benefits of paid employment. State funding and support for infrastructure and technology have been more generous, perceived, as in 1951, as key to national economic growth. This has been perhaps most visible in the slow process of rail renationalisation as well as legal and financial support given to the development of data centres. Most worrying has been the increase of spending on military capacity in a context of global rearmament. This remilitarisation is coupled with an increasing authoritarian and racist drift, exemplified by the proscription of non-violent direct action group Palestine Action as a terrorist organisation and a speech on immigration delivered by Keir Starmer which drew comparisons to Enoch Powell. Popular renderings of 'the spirit of 45' – debunked by many authors I chose to engage with throughout this Element – might make these developments seem at odds with an egalitarian and redistributive vision of Labour. Yet post-war Labour's social-democratic visions of harmony constructed Britain's colonised subjects as separate from the nation's fabric and originated the development of Britain's nuclear arsenal. Labour's policy choices today are also driven by contemporary global contexts and a continued belief in financialisaton inherited from later predecessors; yet analysing more carefully the underpinnings of the post-war social democratic state reveals some ideological continuities between it and the current government. The purpose of doing so is not to directly equate both periods, which would flatten the historical complexities of each distinct moment. Rather, it is an invitation to continue to think beyond a romanticised version of post-war social democratic compact towards horizons that might offer tools to repair the continuing violence of the imperial past and provide renewed versions of collective freedom.

References

59 Productions. (nd). *About Us*. https://59.studio/project/about-us-2/.

Anon. (1951). *Catalogue and Guide, Exhibition of Industrial Power*. S.l: HMSO.

Anon. (1951). *Catalogue and Guide, Sea Travelling Exhibition*. S.I: HMSO.

Anon. (1951). *Catalogue of Exhibits, South Bank Exhibition*. S.l: HMSO.

Ashcroft, R. T. & Bevir, M. (2018). Multiculturalism in Contemporary Britain: Policy, Law and Theory. *Critical Review of International Social and Political Philosophy*, 21(1), 1–21. https://doi.org/10.1080/13698230.2017.1398443.

Balani, S. (2023). *Deadly and Slick: Sexual Modernity and the Making of Modern Race*. London: Verso.

BBC on this Day (no date). *1951: Glasgow powers up for the Festival*. http://news.bbc.co.uk/onthisday/low/dates/stories/may/28/newsid_3005000/3005617.stm.

Bennett, G. (2022). What's the context? The decision to build a British atomic bomb, 8 January 1947. *History of Government*. https://history.blog.gov.uk/2022/01/07/whats-the-context-the-decision-to-build-a-british-atomic-bomb-8-january-1947/.

Beynon, H. & Hudson, R. (2021). *The Shadow of the Mine: Coal and the End of Industrial Britain*. London: Verso.

Bhambra, G. K. (2022). Relations of Extraction, Relations of Redistribution: Empire, Nation, and the Construction of the British Welfare State. *The British Journal of Sociology*, 73, 4–15. https://doi-org.ezproxy.kingston.ac.uk/10.1111/1468-4446.12896.

Bhattacharyya, G., Balani S., de Norhona, L., et al. (2021). *Empire's Endgame: Racism and the British state*. London: Pluto Press.

Blackburn, S. C. (2002). 'Princesses and Sweated-Wage Slaves Go Well Together': Images of British Sweated Workers, 1843–1914. *International Labor and Working-Class History*, 61, 24–44. https://doi.org/10.1017/S0147547902000042.

Blackwell-Pal, J. et al. (2021). Marxist Keywords for Performance. *Journal of Dramatic Theory and Criticism*, 36(1), 25–53. https://dx.doi.org/10.1353/dtc.2021.0037.

Boyle, S. (2024). *The Arts of Logistics: Artistic Production in Supply Chain Capitalism*. Stanford: Stanford University Press.

British Film Institute Archives. (1951). *Mining Review 4th Year No. 10*. 21013.

Buchan, L. (2018). Britain to hold post-Brexit festival celebrating culture, sport and innovation, Theresa May announces. *Independent*. Saturday 29 September. www.independent.co.uk/news/uk/politics/brexit-latest-theresa-may-the-festival-culture-innovation-sport-great-exhibition-queen-victoria-a8561021.html#.

Carolan, V. (2011). The Shipping Forecast and British National Identity. *Journal for Maritime Research*, 13(2), 104–116. https://doi.org/10.1080/21533369.2011.622870.

Christophers, B. (2020). *Rentier Capitalism: Who Owns the Economy, and Who Pays for It?* London: Verso.

Conekin, B. (2003). *The Autobiography of a Nation: The 1951 Festival of Britain*. Manchester: Manchester University Press.

Conekin, B. (1999). 'Here Is the Modern World Itself': The Festival of Britain's Representations of the Future. In Conekin, B. Mort, F., & Waters, C. (eds.), *Moments of Modernity: Reconstructing Britain: 1945–1964*. London: Rivers Oram, pp. 228–246.

Crichton, B. (2015). *Britain's Forgotten Slave Owners*. BBC.

Elliott, E. & Silverman, M. (2018). Rethinking Community Music as Artistic Citizenship. In Bartleet, B. & Higgins, L. (ed.), *The Oxford Handbook of Community Music*. New York: Oxford University Press, pp. 365–384.

Davis, M. (2020). *The Monster Is Here: Avian Flu and the Plagues of Capitalism*. London: Verso.

Department for Digital, Culture, Media & Sport. (2020). 30 creative teams awarded up to £100,000 each for Festival UK* 2022 R&D project. *DCMS*. 16 November. www.gov.uk/government/news/30-creative-teams-awarded-up-to-100000-each-for-festival-uk-2022-rd-project.

El-Enany, N. (2018). *(B)ordering Britain*. Manchester: Manchester University Press.

El-Enany, N. (2019). Before Grenfell British Immigration Law and the Production of Colonial Spaces. In Bulley, D., Edkins, J. & El-Enany, N. (ed.), *After Grenfell: Violence, Resistance and Response*. London: Pluto Press, pp. 77–88.

Franklin, S. (2016). The Context of Forms. *World Picture Journal*, (11). http://worldpicturejournal.com/article/the-contexts-of-forms/.

Gadenne, L., Leroutier, M., Tonito, R. et al. (2024). Air pollution in England reaches 20-year low but inequalities persist. https://ifs.org.uk/news/air-pollution-england-reaches-20-year-low-inequalities-persist.

Geological Society. (nd). *Portrait of Sir Henry Thomas De la Beche (1796–1854)*. www.geolsoc.org.uk/Library-and-Information-Services/Collection-

Highlights/The-Societys-portrait-and-bust-collection/Portrait-of-Sir-Henry-Thomas-De-la-Beche.

Gilbert, J. (2019). This Conjuncture: For Stuart Hall. *New Formations: A Journal of Culture/Theory/Politics*, (96), 5–37. https://doi.org/10.3898/NEWF:96/97.Editorial.2019.

Gilmore, C. & Wilson-Gilmore, R. (2007). Restating the Obvious. In Sorkin, M. (ed.), *Indefensible Space: The Architecture of the National Insecurity State*. London: Routledge, pp. 141–162.

Gilroy, P. & McQueen, S. (2023). *Grenfell Exhibition Guide*. London: Serpentine Gallery.

Goodden, H. (2011). *The Lion and the Unicorn: Symbolic Architecture for the Festival of Britain, 1951*. London: Unicorn Press.

Goodden, R. & Russell, R. D. (1976). The Lion and Unicorn Pavilion. In Banham, M. & Hillier, B. (eds.), *A Tonic to the Nation: The Festival of Britain 1951*. London: Thames and Hudson, pp. 96–101.

Graham, P. (2019). Transnational Digital Biography: The Forgetting and Remembering of Winifred Atwell. *A/b: Auto/Biography Studies*, 34(1), 111–131. https://doi.org/10.1080/08989575.2019.1542827.

Grossberg, L. (2019). Cultural Studies in Search of a Method, or Looking for Conjunctural Analysis. *New Formations: A Journal of Culture/Theory/Politics*, (96) 38–68. https://doi.org/10.3898/NEWF:96/97.02.2019.

Haley, D. (2013). Choir singing 'boosts your mental health'. *Telegraph*. 4 December. www.telegraph.co.uk/news/health/news/10496056/Choir-singing-boosts-your-mental-health.html.

Hall, S. (1981). Notes on Deconstructing 'the Popular'. In Morley, D. (ed.), *Stuart Hall: Essential Essays 1*. Durham: Duke University Press, pp. 347–361.

Hall, S. (2000). The Multicultural Question. In Morley, D. (ed.), *Stuart Hall: Essential Essays*, Vol. 2. Durham: Duke University Press, pp. 95–133.

Hall, S. & Schwarz, B. (2021). State and Society: 1880–1930. In Hall, S. (ed.), *The Hard Road to Renewal*. London: Verso, pp. 95–122.

Hanieh, A. (2024). *Crude Capitalism: Oil, Corporate Power, and the Meaning of the World Market*. London: Verso.

Hendy, J. (2011). *The Festival of Britain: A Whole New World*. BBC.

Hornsey, R. (2010). *The Spiv and the Architect: Unruly Life in Postwar London*. Minneapolis: University of Minnesota Press.

Howells, K. (2021). *The Lion and Unicorn Pavilion: Legacies of the 1951 Festival of Britain*. https://blog.nationalarchives.gov.uk/the-lion-and-unicorn-pavilion-legacies-of-the-1951-festival-of-britain/.

Koram, K. (2022). *Uncommon Wealth: Britain and the Aftermath of Empire*. London: John Murray.

Laville, S. (2020). Air pollution a cause in girl's death, coroner rules in landmark case. *Guardian*, Wednesday 16 December. www.theguardian.com/environment/2020/dec/16/girls-death-contributed-to-by-air-pollution-coroner-rules-in-landmark-case.

Littler, J. (2006). 'Festering Britain': The 1951 Festival of Britain, National Identity and the Representation of the Commonwealth. In Ramamurthy, A. & Faulkner, S. (eds.), *Visual Culture and Decolonisation in Britain*. London: Routledge, pp. 21–42.

Lloyd, D. & Thomas, P. (1998). *Culture and the State*. London: Routledge.

Malm, A. (2016). *Fossil Capital: The Rise of Steam-Power and the Roots of Global Warming*. London: Verso.

Malm, A. (2017). *The Progress of This Storm: Nature and Society in a Warming World*. London: Verso.

Maragh, T., Munroe, A. & Thomas. L. (2020). Grenfell Tower Inquiry – Written submission on behalf of bereaved, residents and survivors. https://gardencourtchambers.co.uk/grenfell-tower-inquiry-written-submission-on-behalf-of-bereaved-residents-and-survivors/.

Marriott, J. & Macalister, T. (2021). *Crude Britannia: How Oil Shaped a Nation*. London: Pluto.

Mau, S. (2023). *Mute Compulsion: A Marxist Theory of the Economic Power of Capital*. London: Verso.

McGurk, S. (2022). Carnival of Brexit: How the Government's £120m 'Festival Of Brexit' Went Rogue. *The House*. Wednesday 31 August. https://longreads.politicshome.com/carnival-of-brexit.

McKie, R. (2020). Did singing together spread coronavirus to four choirs?. *Guardian*. Sunday 17 May 2020. www.theguardian.com/world/2020/may/17/did-singing-together-spread-coronavirus-to-four-choirs.

Meiksins Wood, E. (1999). *The Origin of Capitalism: A Longer View*. London: Verso.

National Archives. (1949). *Festival of Britain 1951 Commonwealth Participation Minutes*. Monday 25 July. British Commonwealth Participation. CAB/124/1220.

National Archives. (1951). *Display of English Language, Lion and Unicorn*. Pavilion. Friday 8 June. Photographic Record. WORK 25/209/D1/FOB3816.

National Archives. (1951). *Official Exhibitions: Exhibition of Industrial Power, Kelvin Hall, Glasgow*. Written Records. WORK 25/3/A1/A4/4.

National Archives. (1951). *Freedom Wall of Lion & Unicorn Pavilion, Location: South Bank*. Photographic record. London. WORK 25/206/D1/FOB-3304.

Norton, K. (2024). What the Pandemic Couldn't Take Away: Group Singing Benefits That Survived Going Online. In Norton, K. & Morgan-Ellis, E. M. (eds.), *The Oxford Handbook of Community Singing*. New York: Oxford University Press, pp. 63–85.

Olusoga, D. (2022). Into the metaverse: My plan to level up Britain – with the 3D internet and a Blackpool 'queercoaster'. *Guardian*, 16 March. www.theguardian.com/culture/2022/mar/16/metaverse-david-olusoga-level-up-britain-3d-internet-blackpool-sheffield.

Our Place in Space. (2022). *Creativity Unboxed*. https://ourplaceinspace.earth/unboxed-creativity-in-the-uk.

Outdoor Arts. (2022). *About Us: Unboxed 2022*. https://outdoorartsuk.org/festival-listing/about-us-unboxed/.

Pickering, P., & Tharpe, G. (1951). The Key to Power. *Mining Review 5th Year Number 1*. (BFI identifier 61098/C-848551).

Read, R. (2020). A choir decided to go ahead with rehearsal. Now dozens of members have COVID-19 and two are dead. *L. A. Times*. www.latimes.com/world-nation/story/2020-03-29/coronavirus-choir-outbreak.

Rifkin, A. (1985). Well Formed Phrases: Some Limits of Meaning in Political Print at the End of the Second Empire. *Oxford Art Journal*, 8(1), 20–28. https://doi.org/10.1093/oxartj/8.1.20.

Riley, C. L. (2024). *Imperial Island: A History of Empire in Modern Britain*. London: Penguin.

RMT. (2025). RMT welcomes skills passport but seek pay and training reform. 22 January. www.rmt.org.uk/news/rmt-welcomes-skills-passport-but-seeks-pay-and-training-reforms/.

Sample, I. (2023). 'A mega-mechanism for bonding': Why singing together does us good. *Guardian*. Friday 15 December. www.theguardian.com/science/2023/dec/15/a-mega-mechanism-for-bonding-why-singing-together-does-us-good.

Seemonster. (2022). Drone Show in Weston-super-Mare. www.youtube.com/watch?v=hDviQer9p2o.

Seemonster. *Seemonster*. https://seemonster.co.uk/.

Shaikh, S. (2020). Could singing be the secret to a more youthful complexion? *The Daily Telegraph*. www.telegraph.co.uk/beauty/skin/could-singing-secret-youthful-complexion/.

References

Shrapnel, D. (2015). From the archive, 4 May 1951: Britain as it might be. *Guardian*. Monday 4 May. www.theguardian.com/culture/2015/may/04/festival-of-britain-travelling-exhibition-1951.

Simpson, J. (2024). BP 'abandoning plan to cut oil output' angers green groups. *Guardian*. Monday 7 October. www.theguardian.com/business/2024/oct/07/bp-abandoning-plan-to-cut-oil-output-angers-green-groups.

Tharp, G. (1951). Mining Review 4th Year no.

The Best in Heritage. (2024). *TBIH2024 IMAGINES, StoryFutures: StoryTrails*. www.youtube.com/watch?v=89R9KvOHlnA.

Toscano, A. (2024) *Late Fascism*. London: Verso.

Tran, M. (2009). Vietnamese shouldn't thank Thatcher. *Guardian*, 31 December. www.theguardian.com/commentisfree/2009/dec/31/margaret-thatcher-vietnam-boat-people.

Unboxed. (2022). *UNBOXED: About Us – Tower of London*. www.youtube.com/watch?v=WqDoUfZEBAk.

Wiles, D. (2011). *Theatre and Citizenship: The History of a Practice*. Cambridge: Cambridge University Press.

Wilson-Gilmore R. (2007). *Golden Gulag: Prisons, Surplus, Crisis, and Opposition in Globalizing California*. Berkeley: University of California Press.

Wilson-Gilmore, R. Keynote. (2019). *Historical Materialism Conference*. Sunday 10 November.

Acknowledgements

For helping this project exist historically, conceptually and materially: Myka Abramson, George Legg, Tom Six, Maria Chatzichristodoulou and Bill Balaskas. Thank you in particular to Tony Fisher and Trish Reid for the suggestion to and support in turning a series of hunches into an Element.

For the reading of sections, invitation and feedback on talks, valuable insights and information and general intellectual camaraderie: Louise Owen, Phoebe Patey-Ferguson, Sophie Nield, Julia Pond, Rob Stearn and PPE comrades Martin Young, Clio Unger, Alessandro Simari, Nicholas Ridout, Shane Boyle and Jaswinder Blackwell-Pal. I have also benefitted from generous insights at TaPRA and IFTR, and Kingston University's Race Gender Matters group.

For comradeship, friendship, and facing storms together: Kirsten Irving, Hannah Ballou, Peter Case, Alex McSweeney, Claudia Haley as well as Layla Renshaw, Martin Dines, Maggie Gray and Éadaoin Agnew. Thank you to Laurie Morue for writing retreat opportunity and to the cows, Saschat and Theodor Catorno for the distractions. Charlotte Floersheim: here's to another twenty-two years of friendship.

Cambridge Elements ⹀

Theatre, Performance and the Political

Trish Reid

University of Reading

Trish Reid is Professor of Theatre and Performance and Head of the School of Arts and Communication Design at the University of Reading. She is the author of *The Theatre of Anthony Neilson* (2017), *Theatre & Scotland* (2013), *Theatre and Performance in Contemporary Scotland* (2024) and co-editor of the *Routledge Companion to Twentieth-Century British Theatre* (2024).

Liz Tomlin

University of Glasgow

Liz Tomlin is Professor of Theatre and Performance at the University of Glasgow. Monographs include *Acts and Apparitions: Discourses on the Real in Performance Practice and Theory* (2013) and *Political Dramaturgies and Theatre Spectatorship: Provocations for Change* (2019). She edited *British Theatre Companies 1995–2014* (2015) and was the writer and co-director with Point Blank Theatre from 1999–2009.

Advisory Board

Aylwyn Walsh, *University of Leeds*
Alyson Campbell, *University of Melbourne*
Ameet Parameswaran, *Jawaharlal Nehru University*
Awo Mana Asiedu, *University of Ghana*
Carol Martin, *New York University*
Caroline Wake, *University of New South Wales*
Chris Megson, *Royal Holloway, University of London*
Collette Conroy, *University of Cumbria*
Freddie Rokem, *Israel Institute for Advanced Studies, The Hebrew University of Jerusalem*
Jean Graham-Jones, *City University of New York*
Mireia Aragay, *University of Barcelona*
Patrick Lonergan, *University of Glasgow*
Rebekah Maggor, *Cornell University*
Severine Ruset, *University of Grenoble*
Ute Berns, *University of Hamburg*
Vicky Angelaki, *Mid Sweden University*
Yasushi Nagata, *University of Osaka*

About the Series

Elements in Theatre, Performance and the Political showcases ground-breaking research that responds urgently and critically to the defining political concerns, and approaches, of our time. International in scope, the series engages with diverse performance histories and intellectual traditions, contesting established histories and providing new critical perspectives.

Cambridge Elements

Theatre, Performance and the Political

Elements in the Series

Theatre Revivals for the Anthropocene
Patrick Lonergan

Re-imagining Independence in Contemporary Greek Theatre and Performance
Philip Hager

Performing Nationalism in Russia
Yana Meerzon

Crisis Theatre and The Living Newspaper
Sarah Jane Mullan and Sarah Bartley

Utpal Dutt and Political Theatre in Postcolonial India
Mallarika Sinha Roy

Decolonising African Theatre
Samuel Ravengai

The Festival of India: Development and Diplomacy at the End of the Cold War
Rashna Darius Nicholson

Theatres of Autofiction
Lianna Mark

Performance and Postsocialism in Postmillennial China
Rossella Ferrari

Staging Class Conflict in the UK
Liz Tomlin

Empire, Extraction and Power in the Festivals of Britain of 1951 and 2022
Caoimhe Mader McGuinness

A full series listing is available at: www.cambridge.org/ETPP

Printed by Integrated Books International,
United States of America